CHILDREN ARE BORN
AND MARRIAGES DIE

CHILDREN ARE BORN AND MARRIAGES DIE

✦

Information "Everyone" Needs for the Best Possible Marriage

Kenn Reese

iUniverse, Inc.
New York Lincoln Shanghai

CHILDREN ARE BORN AND MARRIAGES DIE
Information "Everyone" Needs for the Best Possible Marriage

iUniverse books may be ordered through booksellers or by contacting:

iUniverse
2021 Pine Lake Road, Suite 100
Lincoln, NE 68512
www.iuniverse.com
1-800-Authors (1-800-288-4677)

Because of the dynamic nature of the Internet, any Web addresses or links contained in this book may have changed since publication and may no longer be valid.

The views expressed in this work are solely those of the author and do not necessarily reflect the views of the publisher, and the publisher hereby disclaims any responsibility for them.

ISBN: 978-0-595-44689-6 (pbk)
ISBN: 978-0-595-68905-7 (cloth)
ISBN: 978-0-595-89012-5 (ebk)

Printed in the United States of America

Contents

Introduction

The purpose of this book is to paint a realistic picture of what actually happens to two wonderfully married people before children, and what takes place after children are born.

The objective here is to give the reader(s) the necessary insight and appreciation for **first and foremost** his or her spouse, or future spouse, hereafter referred to as "partner", and to ensure the two of you are doing what is necessary to prioritize your relationship before anything else. Yes, this means even your children. Your children come first in your lives **<u>as a couple</u>**. Nothing short of that is acceptable here. Some will never understand why I've said this. After you've read my book, you will.

The information contained herein is the result and conclusion of documented interviews I've conducted over the past 20 years of my life and is the result of 2,137 independent husband and wife interviews that total 14,959 years of marriage. This is as real as it gets. I've also been married over 20 years.

There are many books out there that are based on psychology and the studies of what side of the brain generates a particular thought or reaction. This is not such a book. This is a compilation of reality, cautions, and tools.

With the divorce rate in the United States at almost 50%, I felt it was important to share the primary reasons why this travesty is affecting so many good people and to provide needful information that will ultimately strengthen your marriage or relationship.

In the first chapter, you will gain a better understanding of why your husband, wife or partner is the person they are today. It will also help you to appreciate them more, and if necessary, help you to provide additional support they may need outside of your ability.

As you move into chapter two, you will realize the differences and extremes that genuinely affect your ability to make decisions. The examples of parents and their differences in chapter two will give you added perspective and create additional room for what you may consider less than acceptable behavior on behalf of your spouse or partner.

Chapter three gives detail of my parents, what they were taught, and what they taught me. The reason for this chapter is to give you an idea of who I am and how I came to be the person I am today. I am by no means perfect. I've endured some of the challenges you will read about in this book and some of the challenges you are facing today.

Chapter four is a tool and mostly tailored towards non-married couples. Called "Compatibility Assessment Tools", it will provide the essentials needed to ensure you are not moving too quickly in your courtship. It will also give you what is needed to make the right decision on whether a particular person is a good fit for you, and it provides specific reason for caution. This is a must chapter for the engaged or dating.

There are many retroactive tools in this book designed to invigorate your marriage. Why are they retroactive? Because, more than likely, you are not doing them anymore, or what's worse, you've probably never practiced some of the tools at all.

Chapter five will examine what used to be, and what's going on today. There, you will gain a great deal of perspective about your spouse after marriage, the importance of nurturing communication, and the essentials needed to keep your marriage exciting and pleasurable. Critical reality is revealed that will absolutely refresh marriages that are one to three years old.

Chapter six will ensure you have a greater understanding of why your spouse or partner is priority one. Whatever you do, don't skip this chapter. The main reason: Your children will leave someday. When that happens, your relationship had better be unified. Establishing core understanding relative to raising your children is paramount. Neither one of you should feel neglected throughout the life of being married with children. Not to mention, many marriages exist until the last child is gone. Don't be a victim of an ever growing statistic.

Chapter seven has the necessary tools designed to establish or reestablish common ground between the two of you. It specifically covers the preteen years and offers tools of discussion and implementation. Children are smart, and will play you against one another if you're not careful. Here you will learn to avoid the dreaded "wedge".

Chapter eight emphasizes the importance of time with your spouse. This important area is generally neglected after children are born and at times to the point one feels very neglected or forgotten. You may not be in this category. That's good. There are many that are, and even worse, a great number of married partners never mention it. This is a sure course to disaster.

Chapter nine emphasizes time with your children. The basic message of this chapter is simple. Either you make the choice to spend the appropriate time with your children, or society and technology will do it for you. The latter will cause you much grief.

Chapter ten will focus on balance, boundaries, and responsibility. Here you will gain a better understanding of why it is so important to embrace these important principles and attributes. Too many children today are of the opinion that everything should be handed to them. While society would have our children believe such mistruths, we as parents are contributing to fallacy when we refuse to hold our children accountable. There is a real cancer that exists in this area of parental responsibility that absolutely cannot be ignored. Boundaries must be set, and consequences must be consistent without idle threats.

Chapter eleven is strictly for husbands and is the result of thousands of comments, concerns and beliefs of wives everywhere. Careful attention should be paid to what is said here. Remember, none of us are perfect, but there are certain things within our control that we could all be much better at. Take time to reflect on the message from our good wives for the benefit of a happy and more complete marriage.

Chapter twelve is strictly for wives and is the result of thousands of comments, concerns and beliefs of husbands everywhere. Careful attention should be paid to what is said here. In order to have a better perspective of how he feels, and how he thinks, please review this chapter. I'm sure it will serve you well in the future.

Finally, chapter thirteen is essentially a reflection of reality, truth, and focus. There will almost always be something in your relationship about him or her that you don't exactly care for. The question is: Did you know this prior to becoming deeply involved? If the answer is yes, and most times it is, then do your very best not to harbor ill feelings towards him/her. Instead, focus on what committed you to the relationship.

For some, this book will shock you. For others, it will edify and enhance your life. If you are married, hopefully you would have read this book before the big "D". If you are not married, this book will prepare you for things to come, and best prepare you for a healthy marriage that will last a lifetime.

1

Understanding Your Spouse/Partner

Firstly, we need to cover the basic make up of our lives to understand who we are and how the personalities of our friends, acquaintances, partners and spouses came to pass. It all starts with our parents.

When meeting new people or new friends, we often wonder almost instantly where they came from. Is he a good person? Why is she always in a good mood? What makes him such a pessimist? All very good questions, but what do we do with the information once we receive it? Do we process it? At that moment we may. Soon after, we're off to the preconceived notions we were raised with, and as we get more involved with that person, their past, their pains, their happiness, we soon forget.

Forgetting is the basic and real conflict of our culture and human nature which sometimes and almost always has caused major problems between two people. Particularly, men and women ... So, where do our parents come into the picture? Let's just say-the beginning.

Our parents, and the parents before them, all have some sort of background which has shaped their lives. Most of our parents have continued with the love and affection, teachings, nurturing habits, bad habits, addictions, neglect, and abuse which have shaped their lives. This trend has transformed you and me to be the people we are today.

We've learned most everything from our parents, and our friends' parents. They have prepared us in a way that has shaped and reshaped the way we think about ourselves, the opposite sex, our friends, and our views on hundreds upon hundreds of subjects. Most of this happens very early in our lives.

We claim to be independent, individual thinkers and masters of our own conscious. But, are we honestly being true to ourselves?

The basic makeup of who we are lies deep within the moral fabric of our teachings and how we were raised by our own mom and dad. For some of us there was only one parent. What about that? For some single parents, it was not an issue at all. For others, it literally tore the family apart.

By contrast, our parents, as well as ourselves, have followed a pattern that has prepared us to function in ways that would affect our relationships for all time. Now, let's explore the different developments and backgrounds of our parents and assess how they might affect our growth and maturity particularly in the early years. The conclusions are applicable to everyone. There are no exceptions.

I will not attempt to cover every sort of upbringing or background. There are too many to explore and the variations of personalities and situations much too vast to cover. However, there are many situations much more prevalent than others or generally more common.

Our personalities are established and created (other than formed by our parents) by living situations and conditions. My friend James was raised by one parent. His mother Susan appeared to be on edge all the time. Susan did her best to manage a job and raise five kids on her own. I could tell even at a very early age that there probably would have been more order if James' father was there. His father left after his baby sister Cheryl was born.

I never knew why his father left, or what really actually happened. I can only say there was a lot of screaming and clothes all over the house on the floors. There always seemed to be dirty dishes all over the place, and the kitchen sink was always full.

Susan would yell and insist the kids did their chores. It never happened though. When James was old enough, he moved out with the knowledge given him by mother, his teachers, his friends, and family. Now, James has been divorced twice, has children from both marriages, and is constantly asking himself what he did wrong.

Honestly, James never really did anything beyond what he learned, experienced, or was taught. In his mind, he did nothing wrong. He could have picked up a few self help books or sought counseling, but either refused to or didn't know help existed. So, James fell into this rut and never emerged from it. This pattern has left him alone and saddened.

Likewise, there are a great number of people and relationships very similar to my friend James. The real problem started in the beginning when a compatibility assessment should have been made. I will cover more about that in Chapter 4. While we could elaborate on his situation at much greater length, I simply want to establish that what James went through in his childhood has had a huge affect on his life and relationships.

Let's explore another. Apart from all the negatives present in our lives are some very good positives. For example, Lucy is a child from a wonderful set of parents with excellent compatibility and understanding. The Smiths' have great balance and respond well to their children. They communicate well and are constantly praising their children.

The Smiths' teach their children to respect others and to be responsible not only for their chores, but for their actions. They have taught the children to love one another and their fellow man as they would love themselves. The children are never talked down to, but are uplifted and confidently encouraged.

That is not the typical family from the conversations I've had. In fact, a rare one, and one in fifteen of the average families I've interviewed over the years. As you think of that, can you imagine the imbalance of the average family? More about that in my next book called **A Society of Pacification**. A rare family like the Smiths generally will raise children that are more considerate of others, more successful, tolerant, and caring. But, what happens when you mix such a balanced child with one totally unbalanced? Sometimes it works out, but most of the time it's just a matter of time before the wheels fall off.

That was the case with my friend James. He married Brea, a lady from a good home with stable and caring parents. Brea could only take so much as did his first wife. James' upbringing was so fragmented. He felt abandoned by his father, unwanted and unloved. I know his mother did her best and she was the best he had.

Does this give you an idea as to how our parents affect who we are and how we are formed? Consider this family ... This is a family of adopted children. Ben, the father, truly feels he loves his adopted kids and is a long haul truck driver. Linda, the mother, is a stay at home mom and very nurturing towards them. When Ben comes home though, he has a different way of showing his kids he loves them. When Ben is sure Linda is resting soundly, his sins begin.

I'm sure you understand where I'm going with this sort of parent. How do you think their children will typically cope when it comes to marriage? His or her virtue has been violated and character destroyed. How well will these children communicate? How much will they bottle up? Is it possible their spouse will become a victim of distrust? Many other factors play into this situation. While Linda has adopted out of love for children, Ben had ill intentions.

The father of these adopted children quite possibly went through the very same thing. Again, a learned behavior ...

Even so, one would think that humans would choose to provide a better life for their child. Unfortunately, these types of violations are not slowing down. Consequently, some children are formed in very unhealthy circumstances as a result.

Now, how about the average parents and family? The average family has a decent home, are two income families, with between one and three children. This average family typically has at least one college grad as a parent with a combined income between forty and eighty thousand dollars. The kids are generally allowed to do just about anything they want and given unlimited freedoms. This is because the average parent generally comes from the same culture as the parent(s) before them.

While it is impossible to cover every sort of parent or background, I wanted to give you an idea of not necessarily where you came from, but where others are coming from, and how it can be difficult to cope. As we move into further chapters, you will have a greater understanding of why this chapter is so important to understand.

2

Aligning Differences

We've covered some of the different types of parents, behaviors, living conditions, and circumstances that make up who we are and some of the reasons why. Now, we will delve into an area that helps us define the decisions we make in our lives. Much of what we learn as children and adults takes place visually. But our views are skewed when we embrace teachings, opinions, or hard core beliefs that sometimes violate personal values tied to such things as <u>The Declaration of Independence</u> or <u>The Constitution</u>. Although there are many subjects to explore which separate and establish our differences, these two have particularly been on trial.

Similarly, our character is partially built upon beliefs based on conversations our parents have had in the home covering unlimited subjects. Although as children we are not often included in such conversation, we recall the opinions. These are the very opinions which then multiplied when your spouse went outside to play years prior to meeting you.

Please keep in mind; this is not an attempt to offend, although in some cases it may.

So, what type of parents did you have? Were they the parents that were very strict? Were they parents that spent much time with you? How about values; were values covered much in the home? Maybe you were born into a very poor family or maybe a rich family. Did your parents teach you to respect your elders? Did they enforce those teachings anytime you slacked off? Possibly, they were parents that over exaggerated the word "freedom" by giving too much of it without reservation.

Either way, you have been exposed by your parents to many subjects and opinions that have given you, in some capacity, the character and personality you possess today. This is not to say we haven't been exposed in other ways. We have indeed. **Only, it all starts in the home**.

Most homes or families are built over the years based on the beliefs of the parents. Take for example the Smith family with values and good moral upbringing. Would this suggest to you that there is nothing negative about them? I think not … We all have our imperfections and damaging views. Needless to say, we all have an agenda and goals, and how we get there or achieve it are almost never two in the same.

Let's explore several types of parental differences that could, has, and would affect our way(s) of thinking and functioning as adults, and imagine the impact:

Extreme Religious Parents: What could be said here? Although a great number of us are religious, there are those whom would base their children's every move, action and decision on their religion. Sometimes to the point, the children have no capacity to think for themselves necessarily. These are the parents that claim to offer agency but actually do not. The children essentially grow up thinking that everything is based on the bible. It really is, but these children need to learn the art of discernment and differentiation, and most of the time, there is little of that in the extreme case.

Growing up in a religious home isn't bad at all. In fact, it is (in my opinion) the best foundation parents can give children as long as there is balance. The amount of free agency given a child would make the difference here. This is where the ability to make a logical decision takes place.

Now, how would the differences in these parents affect the children as they move on into adulthood? Answer ... Their differences relative to religion itself, and the beliefs that, in some cases, cripple ones ability to make decisions outside of their religious beliefs.

Such an extremity is a travesty. Again, in my opinion, a religious foundation is the best foundation parents can give children as long as there is balance. Do as you see fit in your family, as I'm sure you will. I only ask that children are allowed room to grow. A child prohibited is limited in society, and almost always difficult to accept amongst others. Extreme differences can cause a life of pain.

The Poor Parents: Poor can be classified in many ways, but I'm particularly writing about the financially poor and impoverished. Generally, most families suffering hard times are close and protective of one another. This is not so in all cases, but for most poor families, the family is very close. For the most part, my conclusion has shown positive points in this case and negative ones.

Wouldn't you agree that there are a number of reasons parents/families are economically poor? This one is kind of tough really, because you can't place the blame of the parents before them as a means to justify the current conditions of the offspring. At least not entirely ... I have found there are a whole lot of factors that play into poor parents.

Although the factors are limitless, there are some core issues related to why it continues through generations. It has everything to do with the mindset of the parents, the mentality and influence of friends, and even the way a child may view the neighborhood they grew up in. It has absolutely nothing to do with destiny, because being poor can be controlled if managed by optimistic ambition and desire for change.

At the same time, there are those children from poor and impoverished families that refuse to fall into the same pattern or mentality of their respected mother and father. Not because they look down on them, but that they seek more from the positive side of life mentally and financially.

How can poor parents have differences from other parents that will and are affecting their children? Answer ... Their negative opinions and views on life, politics, the wealthy, authority, and most of all, the reason they are poor.

Not all poor parents/families think so negatively. The reasons are endless, and in most cases inbred.

The Financially Secure Parents: The impact these parents have on their children are just as great as the poor parent. All parents for that matter have equal impact. Only the views are different. Mindsets and parental differences in the early stages of a child's life are an integral part of who that child will become.

So, what actually happened that these parents are doing so well financially? Is it simply because someone has to be rich and someone has to be poor to make up society? No ... Somehow, the offspring chose to follow the pattern of success, or create a pattern of his or her own, which resulted in success. The premise of financial security these children learned, were taught, or inherited, gave them the necessary tools needed to prepare for a better future.

Most would believe kids from this type home are very positive, upbeat most of the time, and generally optimistic. I've learned for the most part that this is true. As in any case, there are variances. Actually, there is no full proof system out there for insuring the best for our kids. Although we impact and contribute to the decisions they make based on our differences and opinions, they have a right to choose for themselves the path. Sometimes, it is not what we expected.

Nevertheless, there are values taught in this instance that aren't taught in other circumstances. Financial values that is … Discussions are constantly going on about finances, managing money, or investing it for the future. This is where the family consistency is formatted, thus raising kids that follow very similar patterns of success.

But how do the financially secure parents affect the decisions of their children? Answer … As I said earlier about the offspring, financially secure parents are generally more positive, upbeat and optimistic about life.

We all harbor negative energy to some degree and it is emitted when that nerve is hit. After that, opinions are expressed and generally, if our children are around, they hear it, pick it up, and much of the time will adopt it.

The difference here is that there isn't the worry or living conditions at the level of an impoverished family. Financially secure parents will most probably talk to their children about capitalism. Their views are predominately focused on the safest way to make money and to having the money work for them. They try to teach these things to their kids.

What I don't see happening enough is the message that is given to the children about the less fortunate. A bit more time should be spent on educating their children about their fellow man. During the interviews I have conducted, whenever I've asked the question: Have you taught your children that they are no better than the next person? The answer has almost always been no. Have you taught them to love everyone as themselves? The usual answer is: Not specifically.

Although it is not the responsibility of the financially secure parent to make everything all right in our world, it is their responsibility to contribute to the balance within it, as it is for all parents. This is not to say that it does not happen. It is to say, it does not happen enough.

The Unbalanced Parents: This one is not only a danger to the couple themselves but to the entire family. Chaos limits the children's ability to make a decision for themselves because there are mixed responses, beliefs, differences, and backgrounds. Total trauma …

The unbalanced parent(s) made a very critical error during courtship. They fell in love. Harsh isn't it? I don't mean for it to be harsh. The fact of the matter is, too many relationships are rushed. Physically, human nature takes control of our initial thoughts, views and opinions of the opposite sex at times. When this happens, our real judgment becomes clouded and our ability to focus on what's really important is minimized.

In this case for example, Trish was raised by a good family, medium level income and stable. She was taught by the actions towards her as a child that the consequence for misbehaving was timeout. Trish was never physically disciplined. She learned that politicians are all crooks and can't be trusted and attorneys fall in this category. Her parents complimented her all the time and did all they could to ensure that Trish excelled in anything she did, and if she failed, her parents reassured her that it was all right because she did her best.

On the other hand, Trish's husband Skip was totally the opposite of virtually everything Trish had learned. His decisions were a reflection of his upbringing to the point there were several disagreements daily. As their children grew up, they found that Skip thought it was a good idea to spank as a form of discipline, even though it appeared Trish did not agree with him. He loved law, politics, and debating and Trish did not. Skip told the boys they were men, and should never cry, while

Trish said it was o.k. to cry. If the children failed Skip yelled and Trish encouraged.

It should be evidently clear what this type of combination of parents can do to the decision making development of their children. How can this type difference of opinion affect the children? Answer …

Their lack of good solid communication and refusal to yield to one another's differences even for the sake of the children not only sabotaged their relationship, but the mental stability of the children. Ultimately, marriages such as this usually last less than five years after children are born.

The premise here in this chapter was to give you an idea of a few mindsets that establish differences both between two separate sets of parents of a specific type, the likelihood that your parents were from a different fold individually and the imbalance it could cause because of it. Likewise, it is rare that two people share the same exact background when they are married. Unless certain steps are taken early in the courtship, very serious problems occur especially after the children are born. Believe me …

In some countries, spouses are chosen based on their lineage. The spouses are not chosen by the children but by the parents. This is done to ensure the beliefs of the parents are supported as well as for many other reasons. But, there are never any real guarantees are there? In order to ascertain balance, strengths and weaknesses must be **evaluated and agreed upon unconditionally prior to marriage**. More about that later …

I could continue writing about what makes up parental differences and what causes us to make the decisions we make by covering other parent types, but I think you get what I'm attempting to establish here. There are no particular reasons I chose to write about the different types I did write about. To give you an idea of some others I could have written about, I will list some of them:

- Substance Abuse/Alcoholic Parent(s)
- Physically Abusive Parent(s)
- Mentally Abusive Parent(s)
- Sexually Abusive Parent(s)
- Non Religious Parent(s)
- Society Driven Parent(s)

3

My Upbringing

I feel it's only fair I share a bit of my upbringing with you. This will give you an idea of who I am and what I went through to be the person I am today. Given I've covered a few scenarios for you. After you've learned a bit about my upbringing, you will understand the type of parents I have.

I was born in 1964, in Los Angeles, California at General Hospital to two wonderful parents. I weighed in at nine pounds and four ounces. My Mother said she couldn't get me out fast enough. According to my Mother, I was an eater. I did not like doing much more than eating and sleeping. In fact, I ate so much my Dad put me on junior food at two months of age.

My parents are both educated Black Americans. I am not adopted, but I am the darkest child in the family … So dark that my siblings used to say my Mother found me in a trashcan. For the longest time I believed them. I used to ask questions of my older brother such as, was the lid on the can, or did I turn really dark because the sun cooked me?

I actually didn't take kindly to this story at first. Then, I simply joined in the laughter every time they tried to tease me.

The teasing soon stopped when my siblings realized it didn't bother me anymore. Would you believe I waited until I was around ten before I finally decided to ask my parents if it were true? Little did I know, my older brother had convinced my Mother that it was worth agreeing with him and my younger brother if I ever asked her. Sure enough, she told me I was found in the trashcan. It darn near traumatized me at first, but I was soon laughing again.

Mom didn't allow it to go on for too long though. By the end of the day, she just had to tell the truth.

Including myself, there are four children in my childhood family. My older brother Maco, I share the middle with my younger brother Bobby and our baby sister Angel. We were all very close. We had our fights and disagreements just like any other siblings would, but we were always there for one another. Once our sister was born, we put a very strong protective barrier around her. She's a Leo though and soon removed the barrier when she felt she was old enough to handle boys without our getting involved.

My Mother came from a very strong and deep-rooted family. Grandma was strict and very proper.

Things had to be done a certain way when my Mother was a child. The Lord, respect, honesty, politeness, and cleanliness were on the forefront of her teachings. There were consequences for falling short on chores and for marginal grades. Nothing below a "B" was accepted. She had a routine and Grandma monitored it daily. Grandma was the enforcer.

Mom's dad, Grandpa, was a whole different story. He was laid back and reserved. Grandpa took things in stride. Grandpa was the softy. Make no mistake about it; Grandpa was attuned with the boundaries set for my Mother. According to Mom, they pre-established rules, boundaries and discipline for her before she was ever born and modified them when they needed to. When they argued, it wasn't about my Mom most of the time. It was about something else.

Because of the teachings of my Father, my Mom was put on a pedestal as high as the eyes could see. She is still to this day on that very same pedestal. She has been the lifeblood of the family and always will be. Mom was an only child until my grandparents divorced.

My Father was the oldest of eight children. He was tougher than tough itself. According to him, he had to be when he was growing up. My aunts and uncles endorse this.

Dad's upbringing was much like that of my Mother's. Like my Mother, My Father was brilliant. He was a straight "A" student and excelled in everything put before him. My Dad loved challenges and never turned one down. Not that he won them all, it depended on the challenge, but he was never one to back down from anything or anyone for that matter. I mean that in a very literal sense.

Dad's Mom was just like Grandma on my Mother's side. She was very old fashioned. Her grandparents were slaves and the things they taught her Mother were passed on to her.

The same for her Father, his grandparents were slaves and the deep roots were passed on. One would think this deep root I'm writing about may have a little something to do with hate. Wrong … You'd be surprised … These same teachings were passed on to my Father. I personally believe they are the best teachings I could have ever been taught.

Dad's Mom & Dad had a set of guidelines for him since he was the oldest. They were strict guidelines that kept my Father out of trouble. Grandma was the enforcer. She had eight kids and she didn't play games. When she gave an order, my Dad asked when she would like it completed. Grandpa was the softy. He always knew what was going on in the family even when they thought he didn't, which got some of them into trouble with him. Grandpa never allowed my Dad or my aunts and uncles to play him and Grandma against one another. He was sharp.

My Mother is a nurturer at the fullest explanation. She has always been very soft spoken unless she was really upset. She was always good about picking me up whenever I fell, no matter the circumstance. Mom was best at helping and teaching good moral principals to me from the very earliest of my memory.

I was always one to ask a million questions. I asked so many questions, that my Mom ordered a <u>Time Life Explorer</u> subscription when I was seven years old. It covered everything from insects, reptiles, dinosaurs and more. Soon, I was asking questions about many other subjects. She ordered more books.

Never will I forget my Mothers teachings. She would sit us down and tell us how important it was to respect our elders and to only respond by saying "yes ma'am" when called, "yes, ma'am" or "no, ma'am" when responding to a question. She wouldn't allow her children to respond "Huh?" or "What?" If we slipped, we knew it quickly. Mom was just as firm as our Dad but she had a softer side for sure. At age 42, still to this very day whenever I speak to my Mother, I respond "yes, ma'am" or "no, ma'am" only. And yes, I slip from time to time. When I do my Mom asks, "What did you say?!"

Mom had a routine for us just as she did in her upbringing. We had specific chores to do and we never had all day to do it. She would do the chores with us for the first time and time it. From then on, each chore had a time associated with it. If ever I responded, *"but I have a game in an hour"*, she'd say, "What you have to do should be done in less than 20 minutes, now get it done".

Mom taught us table manners, and family dinners were special. Only one hand on the table she taught. The other hand is used to cut or drink only. You can't finish your soft drink until your food is gone. Never speak with your mouth full. Never pass your hand over the next person's food. Always ask others to pass food you can't immediately reach. You are not allowed to waste food. She taught us the value of food. You have to eat what I cook. You will not prepare something different. Those were Mom's table and dinner rules. Yes, Dad enforced them.

She was very good about making sure Dad was taken care of if he wasn't home for dinner. Anytime that happened, Mom would **first** (before serving us) get a plate and load it up with everything she cooked, wrap it in foil and either put it on the stove top or in the oven depending on when Dad said he'd be home. The same was done if she had prepared dessert. Dad never wondered if dinner would be prepared for him when he got home.

Essentially, Mom was more than a mother to me. She was my friend to. But I never had to guess which came first. She made sure we all knew she was Mom first and friend second. There was a clear line drawn in the sand and we didn't dare cross it. Most of all, Mom was extremely loving and always did her very best for us as we were growing up. I never doubted her care for me. Surely, I slept better each night knowing she did.

Although Mom loved us tremendously, we knew her heart was with my Dad. She didn't make decisions she thought Dad might have a problem with. She was never hasty about much of anything.

I used to always hear my Mom on the phone with friends and family, and I always seemed to be around when I'd hear Mom say, let me speak with my husband **first** and I'll get back to you later. Mom is the same today as she has ever been, solid, caring, loving, a counselor, and on a pedestal as high as the eyes can see.

Dad has always been my hero. I've always looked up to him. He was a strong man. Very strong, mentally and physically. Admired by many, Dad had a lot of friends and acquaintances. As a young boy it seemed we had company at our house quite a bit. Although they'd come over to visit the family, Dad was always the center of attention. He was just a great guy. Everyone loved him. Like Grandpa, Dad was sharp, witty, an intellect, and great communicator.

Although we had a routine, Dad had one of his own. He didn't talk much when he came home from work. He would speak to everyone only if they were in or near the living room. Dad never went beyond it when he came home.

His newspaper was on his recliner and I was assigned to put it there after school. Dad would take off his shoes, recline his chair and open his newspaper. This was a silent time for Dad. When the paper hit the floor, we were all around him.

The things Dad taught prepared me for the world and marriage, and most of his teachings were deep rooted from way back when. Even so, he took great care of us all. He made sure to raise us in neighborhoods that were safe for us. My parents weren't rich, but they did well. Dad was a workaholic at times but for good reason I later learned. Because he was Dad instead of Mom, I didn't ask as many questions. Not that he wouldn't answer them, he was just a bit more serious about everything than Mom was.

I used to love talking to my Dad about what I was going to be when I grow up. He seemed to like that. He would ask me what type of house I wanted and type of car. At the end of every conversation, he reminded me, never stop dreaming son. Never stop dreaming.

The old lessons came from my Dad. Lessons I still believe in whole heartedly and today are teaching my son and daughter.

Dad taught us many things. He taught us boys to respect women. He said women are the best human beings on the face of the planet. Treat them with the utmost respect at all times. Never speak down to ladies in your youth to young girls or as you become a man. You are physically much stronger than them, so be gentle in your tone. Never swear in any instance. Be aware of ladies' feelings as best you can. She has emotions you need to listen to. If you don't, you'll be in trouble.

These are just some of the things he taught us boys. He told us that he learned this from his dad, and that it had been handed down for him to teach us the same. Women were very well respected long ago according to my Dad. As time has past, the level has decreased. Dad told us that would cause problems in the future. With the divorce rate as high as it is, that's a clear sign Dad was right.

Because of my Dad, I always open the car door for my wife. I walk behind her when she walks up the stairs so as to break her fall if she falls, and when we walk down, I walk in front of her.

If ever my parents went for a walk with us, I always noticed my Dad would never allow my Mother to walk nearest the street. He was closest to the street. They held hands wherever they went and it didn't matter where. By watching all this, I learned many things, as my Dad was always affectionate. He was never too manly to kiss my Mom. He did it everyday and so do I with my wife.

His most important teaching he ever shared with us was one about my Mom. One day, Dad came home from work and could hear my Mom whimpering. Once we noticed Dad had heard her, we knew we were in trouble. Mom had just asked us to take care of some things she would generally do herself. She had asked because she was tired. The responses my younger brother gave made her cry. That was unusual of Mom, so we knew something was wrong, and Dad was to be home in just a moment.

When Dad walked in our house and sat in his chair, he took off his shoes and called us all to the living room. My older brother Maco was fourteen, I was ten and my younger brother Bobby was nine. He said, "Boys, that lady you hear crying is my baby, and my baby means the world to me and should not be crying for any reason whatsoever. She should be happy! I don't know what you boys think you have to do to make me happy, but I want you to know you don't ever have to do anything for me personally to make me happy. I'm not interested in you boys trying to please me personally.

You see, your Mother is my life blood. She means the world to me. Your Mother and I are one and we function as such. So, if you want to see me happy, all you have to do is keep her happy. She should always come first in your lives. You will always love us equally if you put her first. If you upset your Mother, then you upset me, and if you upset me, I'll ruin your world …" That day we learned the family golden rule. **Keep Mom happy and Dad will always be happy**.

Dad was always on top of us about our dialect. We were not allowed to speak slang of any sort inside or out of the home. He was taught the same and was himself very well spoken. If ever we came home and attempted to use a new slang, he would put a stop to it quick. Dad explained that it was very important for us (particularly being black) to speak well, and to be well received, we needed to speak as near perfect dialect as possible.

Grandpa also spoke very well from what I remember. Grandpa told my father that speaking well did not make him any better than the next guy and never would he want him to think that was his reasoning.

Dad's reasons were obvious then and are equally obvious now. He told us we could never fully get away from being stereotyped, and because of that, we needed to speak well, particularly during a job interview.

My Father taught us that there was no one in the world better than us and we no better than anyone else in the world. Some will have more money and others less, but that didn't make him or her any better. He said, "People are people no matter the nationality, color or religion. There are good and bad people in every race and from every creed. You can do anything you want in this life. You can be anything you want to be. Always do your best at whatever you do."

We were even cautioned about black stereotypes. Dad didn't endorse nor did he permit racism or prejudice of any kind. We were taught that racism was wrong on any front and that only the ignorant were racist. They (being anyone of any race) were either taught to be, or they were never taught not to be, which is wrong either way according to Dad.

When Dad talked about black stereotypes, he cautioned us to close our ears to the negative past and focus on the future. He asked me a question once that was quite profound. "**How can you walk forward if you are always looking backwards?**" He reminded us never to forget our roots, but that we should press on for the sake of our children and our children's children.

Lastly, my Dad warned, that if after raising us we should ever return to his home and blame our life's failures on any other race (particularly the White American) he would surely kill us.

At age thirteen, I believed him, and I'm glad he said it to us. I'm very thankful my Father taught his deep roots to me. I'm no better than anyone out there, but I am a better person personally because of his teachings. Hopefully, this gives you an idea of who I am.

4

Compatibility Assessment Tools

In the first two chapters, we covered quite a bit about how our parents impact our lives and develop our character. We also covered several different types of parents, and how the differences of those types affect our ability to make decisions both effectively and ineffectively. The reason for this is to help you understand the confusion that can take place when two people decide to become one. The imbalance is generally all right in the beginning because the excitement of someone new overrides what we truly want and feel.

Where is all this leading to? It is leading up to the main purpose of this book which is to explore why marriages die, particularly after children are born and/or have become a part of the marriage. The problem isn't that the child becomes a part of the marriage. It's that the parents feel they have to stop enjoying life to the fullest because of the child. When that happens, death comes to the relationship it once was. Hence, the marriage dies because one or both of the parents all of a sudden forget who they married and why. There appears to be this gap that never was.

The couple is no longer spontaneous. They do not make time for one another anymore or very little if any. Everything comes to a screeching halt. Why? Because a baby was born? That's **not a good reason at all** to neglect one another or your time. Nor is it an acceptable reason to stop doing the things you were doing prior to the birth of your new child. You did and were doing those things (whatever they were) with your spouse because you love it and enjoy it. Now you have to stop? No …

Do you honestly feel you have to do everything with your child or children now? Do you feel you absolutely can't leave your child to a sitter or a family member while you continue to live for a few hours? Yes, even in the first year. What, you feel guilty? For what?! You can't die after children are born. A great number of couples do and they don't realize it.

For those of you that are not married, this chapter will prepare you for the best possible marriage. For those of you that are married and half dead, I will show you how to live again. Read on …

When I tell married people that my wife and I took a trip to Vegas when our son was only fifteen months old, the gravitational pull of what I told them ejects their eyes from the sockets. We had a great time and have since then, again, and again, and again.

When we first meet prospective girlfriends or boyfriends, we have this tendency to move much too quickly at the onset. This isn't to say all people or relationships start out this way, but the majority of them do. It does not matter the bracket of age either. What does happen is (as I said earlier) the physical or external side of that person generally becomes a priority. It is most rare, (particularly in the younger generation) to seek the internal rewards or cautions of the opposite sex.

That said, I will list and explain some of the compatibility assessment tools needed that should be used to determine compatibility before you lock yourself down or go too far in your relationship. If you would do what I'm recommending or would have done anything similar, chances are you wouldn't have gone through the problems you may be currently experiencing in your relationship.

Of course, this does not mean that relationships without such an assessment will not work. On the contrary, if this is done, you will have a much greater chance of having the best marriage possible. At least you will know what you are really getting yourself into. Even with this assessment, things can and will go south, but you will be best prepared for it and the responsibility, if you accepted a long term relationship after the assessment was completed to your satisfaction.

These tools are to assist you and are in no way a guarantee that you will never have issues. There may be other tools of your own needed to complete your assessment. Either way, you will be much better off and will rest peacefully having knowledge of your prospect at the depth of this assessment.

This should be done prior to seriously committing to anything involving you in a relationship, be it a long term relationship without the intention of marriage, engagement, or marriage.

This does not have to be done overnight, but it has to be done over several days or weeks if necessary before you commit to anything. In no particular order, the assessment follows:

Gather Background Detail: Don't be afraid to ask hard questions about them. If they have nothing to hide and are really interested in you, they will answer them non-defensively. Ask very particular questions that will give you information about their family and their upbringing. Allow them to respond. If it appears the questions you're asking are vaguely answered, resort to more specific questions like:

- What is your father like, and what does he do for a living?

- What kind of father has he been to you in your opinion?

- What kind of family did he come from?

- Same questions for the mother.

- How many siblings, and what do they do?

- What is your profession, or what do you aspire to be?

- Are you married?

- Have you ever been married?

- Where did you go to school?

- Do you enjoy sports and attending sporting events?

- Have you ever had trouble with the law or a criminal background? If yes, find out what it is. It may not be substantial enough to write them off. It could be something that scares you. If it is, and you're not comfortable, don't settle. Trouble with the law does not mean they are bad people, but be cautious.

- Do you currently have a boyfriend or girlfriend?

- Have you ever cheated?

- How important are material possessions to you and how is it prioritized in your life?

- Do you feel it is important to personally control everything in a relationship?

Question Their Beliefs: You need to understand the stance or position they take on issues you feel are important to you. Pay close attention to how they respond here. This could be a critical area for you.

- What religion are you?

- Do you have strong opinions about other religions? What are they?

- What are your political views and beliefs? Right wing, left wing—Why?

- What is your opinion of women/men? Why?

- Are you a pacifist, socialist, republican or democrat?

- Are you a bigot? If yes, dig deeper as to why or how it came to pass.

- What is your view of our country?

Question Their Honesty: Very serious area. Be specific.

- What is your opinion about honesty in a relationship?

- What does honesty really mean to you?

- Have you always been honest in your relationships? If not, why?

- Is there anything that has happened in your life that I should know about?

- How do you view dishonesty? How would you handle it?

- What do you believe is the most important part of a relationship?

Question Their Confidence and Beliefs: This assessment is very important because it could cause you a lot of misery early on. Some people carry baggage that scarred them from previous troubled relationships into the new one. Question them to make sure you won't be a victim of unnecessary jealousy.

- What was your last relationship like?

- Who decided to break up? Why?

- What was he or she like? Listen to the tone of the response carefully.

- What did you like about him or her?

- What bothered you most about them?

- Are you one to jump the gun when you can't reach me for some reason?

- Are you possessive? If the answer is no, ask how can you be sure?

- Are you one that worries a lot?

- How confident are you once you're in a relationship?

- Do you often fear losing your companion? If so, Why?

Question Their Respect for Authority and Parents: If you meet someone that has no respect for authority, you are already in trouble. Get out! That same person needs to have a great respect for not only his or her parents but for everyone else's. Depending on what the individual went through with their parents would vary this response. Listen closely, if the word hate comes out anywhere in your assessment, be careful to get an explanation of what is meant by the use of such a harsh word.

- What do you think about our local authority such as the police?

- What are your views on the particular laws? Mention some you feel are important to you and the community. Grade the response.

- Were you taught to respect authority?

- Do you respect your parents?

- Have you broken laws or rules intentionally or just for fun?

- Have you always respected the parents of others?

- Do you call your friends' parents by their first name?

- How do you intend to address my parents? Just curious.

Measure Maturity Level: This part of the assessment must be done to ensure you agree with this person's level of maturity as it relates to you. The same twenty five year old next door may think, process, analyze and resolve at a totally different level entirely. This is not an area per se' that you could ask too many questions about necessarily.

You would have to learn the maturity level by listening and observation. Everything from how they dress to their body language should be considered. Try bringing up certain subjects that interest you. Then watch and listen. You will be able to tell by the tone, how long it took them to respond, the ability to understand your question, and the execution of the response.

Try not to be too critical though. Measure their maturity based on what you expect them to know and even at some capacity what you feel they should know. If there is a conflict in this area, you need to take that into consideration before making a decision on advancing the relationship.

Get Along Well With Others: You need to be creative in finding out whether or not this person has a chip on their shoulder. If he or she does, you need to make sure it's something you really feel you can deal with. You can ask a few questions to help assess this question.

- How do you respond when someone accidentally bumps into you in a crowded area?

- How do you respond to drivers that are discourteous?

- What would you do if someone decided to flip you off during your drive to work?

- How often do you get into arguments with family or friends?

- Do you feel you always have to be right?

- Are you easily angered?

- Do you harbor bad feelings for a very long time?

- Are you a forgiving person?

Question Their Love for Children: Critical! There are too many situations out there that could have been avoided if this assessment had been made very early on. It's important, even if you are not at that level in the relationship where you may feel children are a possibility with this person. Ask questions that are not only important for children, but equally important to you. Do not hold back in this area at all. Be forthright. Again, if they respect you enough, they will have no problem answering your questions.

- Do you like children?

- What are your opinions about children?

- Do you have any children?

- What age is fun for you?

- Would you like to have children?

- When would you like to have children? How soon?

- What do you feel the ideal parent should be like?

- How would you rear your children?

- What types of consequences would you delve out for your children?

- What do you consider quality time with a child?

- What values do you believe are important for children?

- How important is a responsible child to you?

- Do you feel it is important to teach a child service to others?

- How would you prepare a child for racial diversity?

- Do you think it is important to establish boundaries?

Measure Overall Strengths and Weaknesses: Remember, there may be other assessment questions you may feel important to you, and if there are, ask them. Now you should take the time to measure overall strengths and weaknesses. The questions you have to ask yourself are: (Forget about how attractive they are.) Will their strengths compliment you, or threaten your relationship? Will their weaknesses be balanced by you, and are they acceptable?

It's decision making time. Ask—Why am I doing this? Is this a real match for my future? Am I committed to him or her? Should I settle for a maybe? After making your compatibility assessment, your ultimate decision is not only a decision; it is your sole commitment. Remember that ...

5

The First Three Years

So, you've made your assessment and decided to get married. Good! Very good! Now you've taken your first step to companionship for life.

Before you were married, what were the things you did with your new spouse? Where did you go for fun? How often did you go out for dinner? Well, whatever it was, it only marked the beginning of what is to come and you both need to keep doing as much of it as you can as long as you're physically and mentally able.

Let's talk a little about what you were doing just prior to getting married. You had a chance hopefully to get to know one another. You talked on the phone quite a bit before you lived together. You thought about one another all the time. The day could not go by fast enough so you could spend time together. You were courteous and respectful and showed a genuine care for each other and then you became engaged.

Maybe it didn't happen exactly that way, but somewhere within those fibers, you experienced much excitement prior to your engagement. You did everything in your power to impress and you have done well. Your friends have all been consulted during your courtship, and are happy to see you with the person you believe to be the one for you. Some may still have reservations, but that does not matter to you. You knew what you wanted and now you are married.

It was the most anticipated day of your life. You smiled so much it hurt to have a straight face. Everyone was there, your mom and dad, your grandparents, aunts, uncles, cousins and friends from all over the country.

It's a jubilant day, and everyone has had their dance, and you can't wait to set off on your honeymoon. The limousine awaits and as you walk to it, bubbles are blown all around you. From that point on, the journey begins.

This is more of an example of those who could have afforded such a wedding. There are many that simply get married by the Justice of the Peace. I did. Others are married by there bishop, pastor, preacher, sealed in a temple, and even through a drive up window by a Las Vegas wedding chapel minister. The results are ultimately the same and the objective has been met.

Back home to share the beginnings after your honeymoon, it appears nothing has settled the two of you down. You're still smiling, whispering sweet nothings, and having pillow fights. The energy is high between you and there is **nothing** that will bring you down.

You get yourselves situated and work has to disrupt your excitement. It's time to make a living and prepare for the future. There is yet much to explore out there.

The conversations you have are sweet and soft spoken. Both of you are quick to yield to the other when it appears a nerve may have been hit or tensions are in the air. You never leave the house without a kiss at this point of the marriage. You absolutely hate to see her/him go. The words I love you come so easily at this point, and you are anxious to say it. And if you call one another during the day, it's difficult to hang up without saying I love you.

In the first year particularly, you send flowers just because. There doesn't need to be any special occasion, you just do it. Sometimes it's candy. Other times its stuffed animals, but always with a card that says I love you.

The two of you are inseparable and always holding hands wherever you go. It all seems so perfect. When the evening comes you may watch a few shows together, play scrabble, rent movies or even go out to one. Wow, what fun! This is truly the life and there is nothing that could ever convince you otherwise.

At bedtime you are both very aware of your spouses' position in the bed. It doesn't matter which way he/she turns, you turn as well, always close and embracing. What a wonderful feeling. You even dismiss the snoring in the middle of the night. Everything else is fine as long as you are together.

A likely story isn't it? For most, this wonderful beginning has a very short life. In other words, the marriage may last, but the excitement tapers and everything you've read on the last two and a half pages fades quickly. This is still within the first two to three years and many in the first unfortunately. It no longer appears to be the high energy it once was. Sweet nothings are rarely whispered anymore if any at all.

Although the excitement has tapered some, you're both still very happy and doing the things you love. Being spontaneous is fun and enjoyable and it happens often. Vacations are limited but are taken. There are still those times when you take a short drive to visit with friends and family and since there are a lot of them, there are opportunities on just about every weekend. Walks in the park and maybe even exercising are something you both enjoy and an occasional picnic in the sun gives you the opportunity to reminisce.

What you've just read are some of the most common things that happen when two wonderful people decide to get married. Since our economy is ever changing and it is difficult to make ends meet nowadays, couples are less likely to have children right away.

Most newlyweds wait for two reasons. One is to create a savings, and the other is to make sure they have shared ample time together prior to having children.

Much of the time, the decision to wait is not a joint decision. There could be and have been major issues tied to such disagreements. Again, this is one of those questions that could be covered in the compatibility assessment. To enter into a marriage expecting something to happen sooner or later than your spouse intends is quite possibly a future issue that could cause unnecessary friction or worse.

It is very important to talk about children as soon as possible if you missed the "When would you like to have children? How soon?" question. If you do not come to an agreement, at least you're talking about it and getting an idea of when your spouse would like to bring a child into the family. In the event your spouse chooses not to support that idea immediately, please take every precaution to respect her or his wishes.

Oops, I forgot to make sure I was safe the other night story is a bit worn out. I've seen divorce take place because of it. Marriage deserves complete honesty in any situation or instance. Generally, if a spouse is not ready and is told we're pregnant and the wife counted on the husband to be safe or vice versa, there is trouble. Some may stay and some may go, but it usually is never ever the same between the couple.

Marriage is sacred and should not be disrupted. There are exceptions: spousal abuse, child abuse, and others that would warrant disruption if outside resources of support were not sufficient enough to bring peaceful resolution to the couple or family.

Otherwise, as long as there is a relationship where both parties are honest, respectable communication should always be the necessary step that creates peace, happiness, and understanding.

Clearly, there will be other things you may or may not notice during your first two to three years that I feel I need to make you aware of. The reason for sharing this with you will help to do one of two things for your marriage: Restore what was once there, or if you are not married yet, prepare you to be mindful of the pitfalls that will drain the life out of your relationship or marriage.

Remember all of the wonderful things I covered on the first few pages of this chapter? Well, how much of the beginning of my courtship and marriage would you think is still actively taking place? Answer … All of it.

Since I was a kid, I watched, listened and learned. Just like anyone else would. I was very selective with what I adopted and what I would consider unloving behavior on my behalf. My Father treated my Mother as if she were the Queen of England. He opened the door and pulled out the chair for her at every possible opportunity to do so. And, he spoke gently. He was, in my opinion, the most considerate of all, especially in regard to my Mother. I adopted the same behavior and respect.

I wrote about all of the excitement in the lives of two people in the beginning of their relationship and how (after what I would consider a very short period of time) the average relationships tend to fade quickly away from such a wonderful start. This is because the level of excitement wears off like a pair of well worn shoes. It doesn't have to be this way. The question I would like to ask is: Were you pretending in the beginning? I didn't think so. The conversations that took place had a lot of praise and thankfulness.

What happened? At the start, there was praise that told her/him that they meant everything to you, and that you absolutely could not see yourself living without them. You both were thankful that the two of you met, and felt there was no way there could ever be life without each other. Now things have changed. As time has past, there have been some observations that are not entirely pleasing. New discoveries maybe?

Things have appeared to slow down too. The spontaneous trips hardly ever happen. The cuddling seems uncalled for anymore. Now you sleep on the other side of the bed and hog the covers. Laughter presents itself but with much more effort. The flowers no longer come. Movies happen ever so often. Particularly with the male, "I love you" seems to be the hardest thing to say. Needless to say, it is by far the most important.

If you can also recall earlier how I mentioned our human inability to get involved with someone based on more than their physical appearance and the unfortunate high emphasis put on it. This saturates the probability of future issues of which you may be experiencing now. Did he/she stop going to the gym? Maybe gained a little weight around the waistline? Now what? The image has changed for you? Are you telling yourself this is not what I married into?

How about the way you communicate with one another; how is that going? Are your conversations no longer gentle and soft spoken? Is your spouse getting upset because he/she feels you are suggesting they've gotten a little chubby by constantly inviting them to go to the gym with you? The two of you used to yield to one another for the sake of argument. You found ways to compromise and work through things amicably. Now, winning the argument is the only end result all of a sudden. Then the silent game takes position between you.

What's worse is the fact there aren't any children yet. The foundation built between the two of you not only has to be solid, it has to be unified. At this point and time in the marriage or relationship, if you do not have excellent communication and problem resolution skills, you are in for one big surprise when baby comes.

The baby (when it arrives) is one of the main reasons for this book. The next reason for this book is to prepare you for the baby by doing my very best to ensure you both are doing what is necessary to have the best possible relationship through simple communication prior to the baby's arrival. The most important reason is to make sure you functionally stay alive after the baby is born and are doing everything you were doing when you first met. The only exception should be limitations of finance, but do not fall into the trap of using finance as the excuse.

Couples who are not prepared or are not supremely unified in their direction are doomed when the baby comes. Many have this impression that the baby will bring them closer together. Not necessarily true. One would believe that it would, and from the moment it arrives, it usually does bring this unified feeling. Don't be fooled by this feeling. Your ability to outline and agree to how you communicate, deal with finances, recognize strengths and weaknesses, and agreeing to what you accept and do not accept are paramount.

This absolutely has to be done between the two of you. No exceptions! If in fact exceptions are made, and you overlook an issue or problem that needed working out, it could tear the relationship apart. I am not perfect either and have made mistakes. I am not afraid to admit it and I'm always doing something to better myself and my marriage. I could never tell you that I know it all. I don't.

But my research and twenty years of marriage is not the norm, and experience gives me the down-to-earth essentials needed to help make your relationship or marriage the best you could hope for.

First, if you are not doing the fun things you were doing when you first met, start doing them again. If finances are low, choose to do low budget things. One way to keep this up is repetition. You've heard the saying, the more you do something the easier it becomes. Then it will become habit and that is exactly what needs to happen. So get started this week. Commit to it now.

My wife and I regularly have date night every Friday night. We did it before the birth of our first child and we still do it now, and yes our children are still living at home.

We go out on Saturday night too and sometimes during the middle of the week. All morning Saturday and all day Saturday, we are with our children and the entire day Sunday. During the week our kids are with us Monday through Thursday. When I get home from work, all friends have to go. We eat together, read a story as family, do something individually for personal progress, pray together as a family, hug one another and prepare for bed.

Now, I will give you the tools needed to help keep your marriage solid and establish a relationship of unification. As stated in the "Compatibility Assessment" chapter, these tools are to assist you, and are in no way a guarantee that you won't have conflict from time to time. I can personally promise if you apply these principles, adopt them into your lives and practice them, always having a sensitive conscious for the welfare of your relationship or spouse, your relationship will not die when the children are born. I promise you that.

Where do you think I come in my wife's life? If your guess was **First**, you are right. Our children are First in our lives "as one unit". To us as a couple, "we" put our children first. We function as one and our children understand this. How? My wife and I are unified and have established a foundation that is solid. One that keeps **us happy First.** If we are unhappy, the children are affected negatively. We have taken the teachings from our parents that we felt benefit us most, applied them and it works.

Here are the tools I promised in no particular order:

Personal Commitment: You must absolutely recommit yourselves to one another. I'm not saying you're not committed. I'm suggesting the commitment has faded. To be committed is a great deal more than the wedding ring on your finger or the fact you said I love you two weeks ago. It has other meanings like faithful, devoted, loyal and dedicated. The way you personally perceive this meaning is very important.

Part of this commitment is to say I love you with meaning, real intent and feeling. I say it several times a day. Although I do not expect you to say it as much as I do, I do believe it should be said at least once a day at a minimum. The ultimate message here is to give of your full self, not just today, but all the time. There is absolutely no reason not to.

Compliment Often: It is so important to do this as you once did at the start of your relationship. Things were always said that lifted you up, and if you entered into this relationship with a low self-esteem already, you really deserve to be uplifted and so does your partner. I don't really need to put words into your mouth here. It's simple and it means a lot. Take notice, and make it a point to compliment while you're at it.

Safe Haven: Critical … In order for anyone to communicate effectively, there must be a feeling of safety in the relationship. Safe to say what is on your mind at anytime without aggressive retaliation. No one likes walking on eggshells, and it is not healthy for the relationship. Threats of physical abuse are a clear sign of trouble. Physical abuse has no place in your relationship. There isn't a safe haven in such a frightening situation. If you feel threatened, make sure your partner is aware of it. Feeling safe is a very critical part of having a healthy relationship.

There should be comfort in knowing you can communicate without mental manipulation or physical abuse by either party. If there has not been a safe haven in your home, create one now.

Focus on the Positive: My wife years ago would tell me I commented on what was wrong more than on what was right. It hit me hard when she said that. This was another turning point in our relationship. I've always said—Surely the good outweighs the bad. Focus on what is good in the relationship. Do it often. I'm not saying ignore things that bother you. Communicate those as deemed necessary, but try your best not to nitpick. Love your partner positively and in every respect you can imagine. Always think about what is going great in your relationship. If you do this, I promise increased happiness beyond measure.

Financial Crisis Support: Extremely important! There have been and are major problems in this area. Many arguments, disagreements or worse take place because of finances. Do not allow this one to drag you down. One specific vow I remember is, "For Richer or Poorer". We all have ambitions and goals in life. No one ever knows what tomorrow will bring. When times get tough, support one another. Speak reassuringly …

You should never want to have your partner believe money is of more importance than they are. Please do not do that. Once you're stable again, you may lose them, maybe sooner. Do your best to avoid arguments about your financial status. You made a decision to be together. I hope you did it unconditionally.

Listen, and Listen Well: Sometimes, we have a tendency to "jump the gun" and assume our partners are saying something they really are not. I've done this my fair share. It's important to listen and to listen well.

The perfect way to do this is not only to listen attentively, but to refrain from taking it personally. Even if you feel you are being attacked verbally, keep good eye contact, making sure your facial expression is not defensive, but neutral.

Many times our partners merely want to talk or express their feelings or impressions about something or someone. It's not always you they want to address. This is where assumptions tend to be dangerous. Never should you be in a rush to speak. Human nature (particularly on behalf of men) is to fix everything. I implore you men to delete this way of thinking immediately. Women are generally very good listeners. If your wives want you to fix something, they will be very specific about it. Patience is a virtue to those that practice it on themselves. Listen, and listen well.

The Power of Reflection: Use this tool anytime you feel you need to talk about something that is bothering you. The outcome of your conversation will almost always be a good one.

To use reflection, you must be a good listener as well. Here's how it works: Ask your partner or spouse if now would be a good time to speak to them about something without interruption or until you say you are done. If the answer is yes, sit down and express your feelings. After that, what has been said is now repeated back to you to make sure they heard you correctly and to ensure they understand what you're saying. Then confirm whether or not they got it.

Then allow them to tell you how they feel about what you've just said. Thereafter, you need to be the listener and reflect back what was said to you. At this time you've both established your feelings. Settle up by meeting half way at a minimum if nothing at all. When disagreements get to the point no one is really listening, try the power of reflection. You'll be glad you did.

Have Fun: The fun should never ever cease no matter what. Be as spontaneous as possible. Go out to a friend's house together for a visit or two. Laugh more and enjoy yourselves to the fullest.

6

Marriage with Children

At this point in your lives, I should only hope you've prepared and planned well. There are a great number of discussions you should have had prior to having any children. I don't mean conversations about having a child. If you do not have any children, I will provide the discussions you should cover.

If there are children in your lives, even as a result of adoption or marriage to someone that already has children, there are discussions that should have already taken place. If not, what I will cover here will give you an idea of what you should do, especially if there have been arguments that are **"In Your Opinion"** because of the kids. Nope, it's never because of the kids. It's because of you and the way you've chosen to deal with it. Arguments may be about the children, but never because of the children.

This is the time (after the baby is born) when marriages generally die. This is generally the point in married lives where you forget who you married and why. All the reasons for loving your spouse become somewhat tainted. Your spouse is no longer a priority in your life. Time together dissipates ridiculously. Everything appears to change dramatically. The word neglected surfaces all of a sudden. You've forgotten that there's enough love for everyone.

The fact of the matter is you just have to learn to balance that love. There will be slight adjustments in your sleep schedule, but the activity levels in your lives should never slow down to a crawl. The first year requires more of you, yes. Do not abuse the excuse. You can't afford to.

It is extremely important that you never forget who you married and why. Many of you are asking; how could I ever do that? It's not that it's done intentionally.

In most cases it isn't realized by the offender. That could be dangerous especially if your partner elects to seek attention outside of the home. No, I'm not advocating it. The interviews I've conducted over the years have shown that seeking attention outside the home becomes a self-justified option "when one feels forgotten or neglected".

Take this seriously. Just because your spouse is an adult does not mean they are no longer human. Male or female, sometimes the decisions people make due to a change in circumstance or situation isn't plausible. This is another reason **your spouse comes First** in your life. Your children are first to you as one unit or as a couple. Not only must you think this way, you must function this way if you want the best marriage possible.

Your spouse should always feel the same level (if not higher) of love from you she or he has always felt prior to your new child or children. Tainted love is easily recognized by the recipient. Be cognizant of your spouses' feelings. Make sure to keep your partner or spouse a priority by balancing time between your children and you.

Yes, I know the children need more attention from time to time, but you have to give equal time to the one you married. Don't make excuses! My wife and I still make plenty of time for one another and we are very happy because of it. Take my word for it; I've only been married twenty years!

Be prepared. Take the necessary steps to ensure you are both comfortable with the way things are going to be. Establish a clear understanding of when you will do things together and with your children.

It is very important at this point to understand your combined position. If you are communicating well, there will be little chance that confusion will beset you. Focusing on the positives within your relationship will keep you jointly happy while also providing the tools necessary to recognize a probable wedge.

Always remember how it all started. It didn't start with you and the children. It started with you and your spouse. That's how it should always be. Nothing should ever come between you or wedge you apart. Nothing! Not even your children. Be careful to remember that. Forever ... Raise them together. This is not an individual role.

The following are the discussions I mentioned earlier. Here, you will have an opportunity to understand why these discussions are important and how utterly conducive they are to your marriage. Again, if you are not married, dating, married with or without children, these discussions will better prepare you or assist you immediately no matter the status. Essentially, these discussions will (particularly after the baby is born) assist in keeping your marriage or relationship healthy and alive.

This is not all though. There is much more to absorb in this book that will strengthen your marriage. Reread this book and absorb until it becomes a way of life.

These discussion points are in no particular order. I will leave the content of theses discussions to you. Just make sure you cover it. Ask questions until you feel comfortable that as a couple you agree. Once you've done that, stick to it. It will work out after the baby is born **as long as you are consistent.**

What Type of Parents Should We Be? This is a discussion that may seem meaningless. It's not, I assure you. You may have an idea of what type of parent you will be, but are you sure your spouse is on the exact same page you are on?

At the start, you want your spouse on page one with you, not page thirty two. Unfortunately, that happens too often and leads to a much unexpected road you never anticipated.

What Things Will We Teach Our Children? Have a very important discussion here. This will surely encompass several detailed areas of interest on the part of both parties. A really good thing to do here is to create an outline between the two of you. Outline the things you feel parents should teach. Most of this is natural, but different backgrounds could yield teachings you do not agree with. Make sure to agree on what is taught.

There are many things your kids will learn from the outside. There is not much you can do about that. Surely though, there are very particular subjects only you should teach the children. The task at hand is to prepare them for society, responsibility, accountability, people, and the world. This will vary in age for your children.

Some mature faster than others intellectually. You may have your second child reach age nine and may not be prepared to learn the things your first child learned at nine. Be prepared to make adjustments if needed.

It is never wise to attempt to force feed one child because the other one learned, picked it up, or understood it better. Teach them at their pace. Again, there will be many subjects to address. Most parents discount such teachings and when they attempt to make corrections later, it's too late.

Responsibility and Accountability: This is also a very critical area in your children's lives, and the way you handle it will structure a lifelong pattern. As you converse about this, make sure you both agree to incorporate responsibility and accountability very early in your children's lives. The earlier the better ...

Many parents I've interviewed with told me they started as early as they felt their child would understand. One example is to have them (between the time they start walking and age one) help you put their toys away after play. When doing this, talk to them and explain the importance of being neat and orderly. If you start early enough, they will always remember.

At the same time, both parents must absolutely be on the very same page. In order to do this, you must be consistent without exception. No one ever said raising children would be a cakewalk, just in case no one ever told you. In other words, if you decide to create a new rule for your children, both parents must consistently enforce it. If one child or all take notice of imbalance on the part of the parents, there will be a disruption between you, and even worse a possible mutiny which will be used against you, because of your inconsistency.

There are many parents that fail in agreeing much after this discussion, because one would rather be a softy. It's all right to be soft. There will always be one parent softer than the other, but that is not an excuse to be inconsistent. Maybe because they feel the children won't love them. I really don't have the answer for you particularly because there are so many excuses or reasons I've discovered. What I can say is, don't worry. Children will respect you more if you are consistent. It does not mean you do not love them.

The unity exuded between you will be a huge factor in how your children view your relationship and the solidness of it. As a couple, you must function as one.

Respect: This is another area I think is almost totally lost in our society today. If you believe that the world is a no boundaries playground and respect is overrated, you should skip this discussion. It will haunt you like the plague in the near future. The claim that you are happy without teaching respect is fabricated. Your children will trample you, and your decision to not teach respect because you feel no one else is doing it, or because no one taught you respect is a liability you will regret. In my next book **"A Society of Pacification"**, I cover this neglected need of **respect** in much greater detail.

For those of you who understand the value of respect, I commend you. This discussion between you should be taken seriously as in any other discussion. Society has become extremely self-removed from respect, and teaching respect to your children won't change society entirely, but it will help create a new generation of respectable youth.

Everything had to have a beginning. The equal rights movement was not a success overnight. The mission to the moon was at first an idea, a vision and a dream. Now, it is a reality. We can have the same idea, vision and dream for having more respectable children.

Not all children are disrespectful, just the majority. How many of your children's friends address you by first name? Why do you allow this? Is it allowed because you think it makes you feel old being called Mr. or Mrs., sir or ma'am, or is it because it gives you the feeling of being accepted by the youth? Hogwash! We are **Parents' First** people! We do not have to feel accepted by anyone, especially someone else's children. So what if you're forty years old, it doesn't mean you have to feel forty. You're only as old as you feel and if being disrespected is your antidote for feeling younger, what a travesty for the message you are sending to your children and our youth. Rise above it, you deserve to be respected. Period!

Honesty and Integrity: This is something that should be handled by example and careful observation, particularly in the early stages of a child's life. In other words, it is important that you are cognizant of what is going on in the daily life of your child. This means you have to pay close attention to what he or she is doing. If you ignore intentional lies and deceit and rationalize wrongdoing, you are headed for destruction. Too many parents I've come in contact with use excuses such as: "Oh, he's just a boy!", or "Oh, that's what all the kids do". This type of mentality will soon self-destruct.

Get involved and become a part of your child's life implicitly. After picking them up from a dance or a movie with friends, give them an opportunity to tell you how things went. Observe each of these opportunities several times without speaking of your observation. Then, if you conclude that not once did your child ever share his or her outing with you, you may want to enquire. It's one thing to be secretive, and another to be hiding something that could possibly be harmful to them. If they are willing to share their day or outing with you, you have a better chance of helping to keep them safe if necessary.

The rest of what they learn about honesty and integrity will take place when certain decisions are made in their lives. You can only teach so much. Again, a great deal of this teaching will come from the example you set for your children in the home. They are watching you and will be paying very close attention to what you say versus what you actually do. Because of this, it is imperative that there are no such things as idle warnings of consequence in your home. Follow through, and be consistent, and honesty and integrity will be taught effortlessly.

How Will We Show Love? Although one would believe this would come naturally, it is again one of those areas that need to be discussed. The approach to this is different in some individuals prior to getting married due to their personal upbringing. Remember chapters one and two? Those chapters justify this discussion. Even though (if you are reading this prior to marriage) you've completed a compatibility assessment, you still need to make sure, especially prior to the birth of your new child that you both have the same beliefs in this arena. If not, iron them out and compromise.

One couple I talked to thought that it was all right to chastise their children by yelling and screaming at them. This same couple also thought there was nothing wrong with calling them names like "stupid" and "worthless". Because of the parents' upbringing, this was how they showed love and believed it was all a part of the process. That was their validation. Make sure that you both agree with how you speak to and communicate with your children. I beg that you will. The conversations between your spouse and child could very well shock you. Be prepared.

None of these discussions will make things perfect around the home, but if taken seriously, agreed upon and established over time, there will be peace and happiness.

How Much Television? There are many excellent education programs on television today. There is also a plethora of trash television out there. Children as well as adults are merely a product of their environment. What they see and hear is very critical, especially in the early stages. This area becomes hard to control when they visit friends, but if you share certain cautions with them early about particular content and or things to avoid, and assure them that you trust them to make good decisions while away from home, they will do as you say more times than not.

You can't wait until they are twelve to teach them this though. The best thing to do here is to be an example. It all starts in the home.

Values: This discussion should include everything involving your points of view on principles, standards, ideals, ethics and last but surely not least, morals. Of course, there will be stages in the life of your children you feel would be most appropriate to discuss this. Still, it would be a great idea for the both of you to discuss when this should happen. It doesn't have to be laid out all at once. It could be done once a year just prior to your child's next birthday. As they advance and mature they will be ready and you will know best when to discuss/teach certain values.

If you choose not to or dismiss the importance of teaching your children values, don't worry, society will teach them for you. If you can live with that, you can skip this discussion.

Discipline/Consequences: Agree here or fight constantly. Your choice … This is an area I've found has, will, and does have a huge affect on the relationship of husband and wife. Really discuss and talk this one through thoroughly. Make definitely sure you are both in total agreement. This is a broad range conversation. Discipline and consequences vary and broaden over time as the children get older. Don't tamper with this discussion. I've seen the big "D" take place because of it.

These are the essential discussions I feel you should have prior to having a child and there are many others as well that you may come up with. The reason these discussions were chosen is because I have found that these are the areas that most drive a wedge between two wonderful people and at times end in divorce. Don't become a victim of ignorance. Do everything possible to be aware and educated. Keep your marriage alive. In order to accomplish this, you must realize the importance of putting each other first.

7

Establishing Common Ground

Apart from everything else we've covered, there are several other elements of your marriage that need to be taken into account regarding yourselves and your children. There are in fact some precautions that will establish common ground between the two of you. This common ground I'm referring to is the unity and solidification I spoke of earlier. Once again, it is absolutely imperative that both of you function as one. The early stages are those years prior to teen years, and if you are made aware of or address these precautions prior to the teen years, and prepare yourselves to function as one, everything will run much smoother in your family.

From a baby until the time your child can talk, you will be tested. Initially during baby stage, patience will be required.

When the walking starts, the cooing dissipates and actual words began to come forth. Generally when this happens, most fathers have no idea what the baby is saying and has to ask the wife to translate for them. For some reason, moms just know. Call it mothers' intuition.

Remember, children learn a lot by what they see and hear. I will offer some key points of caution for you and then offer up some things to look out for. Particularly the wedge ... My main objectives in this chapter are to make sure you **avoid the wedge** and to help you to prepare for the early stages by also reminding you to avoid certain behaviors. These simple practices and cautions will increase communication, understanding, and keep order and peace in the home. Essentially, as you establish common ground, you'll set the standard as well.

So, when we are in the presence of our children, speaking around our children, or performing certain functions in the presence of our children, we need to really pay careful attention to our behavior.

These are cautions that some of you may already be aware of. On the other hand, there are the many backgrounds that justify the purpose of making sure this awareness is mentioned here. In other words, some of these behaviors may be acceptable for some based on their upbringing. If you honestly care about how what you say or do affects your children for the balance of their lives, you will pay close attention to these early stage behavioral cautions and warnings. They are as follows:

Never Argue in The Presence of Your Children: Again, they watch and listen to you. Although it is important your children see you as humans, try to avoid arguing in the presence of them as much as possible. It's all right if they notice a mild disagreement from time to time. That helps reassure you are fallible people and parents. At the same time, if a mild disagreement does take place, make sure they are also a part of witnessing the resolution. This will create balance in the standard of dealing with disagreements for your child. He or she will learn this art from you.

If there are ever any heated discussions between you, make sure to take this somewhere else. Having children witness extremely volatile arguments gives them permission inadvertently to do the same. To them, it's a way of life because they learned from the best, their parents. So, if this is something you currently do in their presence; don't get upset at them for doing it with their siblings. You've basically given them a free ticket to handle things that they don't like very aggressively.

It is my sincere hope that this does not happen in your home. If it does, please try to handle your displeasures calmly. It will have a much greater impact on your children's problem resolution skills in the future.

Mind Your Tone: There is some mystery about how a child responds to the voice of a father versus that of a mother. Particularly in the early stages, your tone should be as normal as possible when communicating with one another. As your child grows older, there will be times that you will need to vary your tone for corrective reasons. In the meantime, do your best to keep a normal tone. If your tone comes across too firm too often, you'll create an environment of fear. When I was a child, I could tell distinctly who was talking because of the tone difference of my Mother and Father.

Everyone I've interviewed has said the voice of their father always appeared more commanding. I personally believe that is naturally true. Because of this difference in tone, most of us responded to our fathers' orders immediately. For this very reason, especially for fathers, mind your tone. Allowing your children to get used to your normal voice will be most helpful in the future when they began to test your skin cloth. Varying your tone is good because it sends several different communication messages to them.

At the same time, be mindful in this early stage. You do not want them to grow up afraid of you. You will want them to talk to you and to confide in you. If your tone is such that there is no feeling of safety between you and your children, you will miss out on a whole lot. Don't make this mistake. I'm not asking you to be perfect. I know by experience how hard it can be to remember and to always be cognizant of your children's whereabouts when communicating with your spouse. I also know that practice will bring us that much closer to perfection. Work on it as best you can.

Mother, Father and Parent before Friend: This is a huge caution to remember and ultimately one of the most important. Many parents struggle because this is not something realized in the early stages. Too many parents today are more focused on being a friend to their children. Huge problems can and most often do occur because of this mentality. It not only causes problems personally, but problems between you and your spouse will multiply twenty times over. I cannot emphasize enough the issues that will result from this thought process.

Friends; your children will have plenty of them. There is no need for you to feel left out because you don't speak the same slang or lingo, wear the same clothes, or have the same piercing or tattoos that your children suggest make you more hip.

Your objective is not to be their friend first, nor is it at all necessary to look or feel cool just because your child believes that is what is best for you. What? You fear being a parent first will move your child further away from you? Get real! The opposite is true. The problem we face here is there are too many parents focused on what they can do to please their child. There needs to be more parents willing to ask themselves—what can I teach them that will make them more responsible and self reliant?

There are far too many cases today where children of every age from eighteen to forty five are returning home to their friends financially or otherwise. Notice I said returning home to their "friends". Parents will make sure to place responsibility and accountability as a high priority in the lives of their children. Parents are going to make decisions that are right socially, ethically, and morally first.

Parents will be the first to realize that you can have fun and enjoy the life of your children by being a parent first. Bottom line, you can make solid decisions if a parent is at the forefront of such decisions. Being a friend first will cloud your judgment and ability to make parental decisions.

Be Positive Towards Your Child: Extremely important ... Many children are raised in families where they are abused by the things said around them, and even more damaging are the things said to them. It is extremely important that the comments made to our children are positive and uplifting. As their parents, they naturally expect us to be positive and uplifting unless you change that expectation. Later in life these children, now adults, will be more positive, confident, assured, and optimistic.

Do your best to agree never to belittle them. Yes, there are times when you will need to speak constructively to your children. Even then, make sure (even if you are disappointed about something) to communicate in such a way that isn't aggressively demeaning to them. Express disappointment in a very gentle way and with a smile, but have twice the positive comments during that same conversation.

Do Not Compare: Not only will this cause a problem and establish resentment between your children; it will cause resentment towards you. Remember, every child is different and gifted in their own way. No two are exactly the same and they never will be. Accept each child for their own personal growth. Some children mature faster than others. Some children love to read. Others don't. Some children are tidy and organized. Others may never be. If you are consistent in keeping up with them, they will progress nicely.

Comparing your children will scar the relationship between you and the offended. If this was a practice of your parents, drop it immediately. It will not help your family. Children want to feel accepted for who they are. As their parents, we should want to do our very best at ensuring they know we love them just as they are. This doesn't mean there are no boundaries or consequences for their actions. Not comparing simply means you care about their feelings and individual worth.

Avoid The Dreaded Wedge: This should not affect your marriage in the early stages. If there is a wedge, the both of you are to blame. The workings of your child are not mature enough to contribute at this time. As they grow older though, the both of you should be mindful of what is being said between your children and your spouse. If you both are working together as one unit, you should not have much of a problem here. The fact of the matter is most parents do not function as one unit.

The wedge in my opinion is an act or a game played against you by your children. On one hand you are told one thing and your spouse is told the opposite. This is of benefit to the child. If he or she can get the both of you to clash in some way or another by playing you against each other you're doomed. Next thing you know, you are arguing with your spouse. Later you find out what really happened and the ulterior motive your child has conjured up. By that time, it's simply too late. The damage has been done.

If I went to my Mother and asked for something and was told no, I knew not to go to my Father and ask the same question. How? I knew my parents were well in tune with one another. The first question out of my Dads' mouth would be, "Did you ask your Mother this question already? If so, what did she say?" After my response, my Father would ask me if I was sure my Mother said those specific words. I had to make sure I did not fabricate my Mothers' words. Dad was sure to confirm them with her before offering an answer to my question. Furthermore, he always followed up with Mom afterwards. My Mom did the same.

Essentially, these cautions are here to assist you if this is your first child and to also prepare you for future children. In the early stages, be mindful of these and others that you may feel need addressing. I really believe that these cautions are beneficial to the overall upbringing of your child and should not be taken lightly.

Common ground is created when both parents agree to how they will handle and address certain issues or concerns that arise or may arise when children are born.

You may not cover everything. Surely you will miss something. That should not be a problem. Once discovered, you'll know what to do. Whatever you do, always discuss things involving family with your spouse. Never leave him/her out of a decision you've made for the children. If you do, big trouble awaits around the corner.

8

Time with Your Spouse

Indeed, there is a reason for this chapter being first before the next topic. Most of you might believe the chapter before this one should be "time with your child". Nope, that chapter is next. Why? Come on, you haven't forgotten already have you? Your spouse is priority one, first, primary, foremost, and was and still is the initial one prior to your children which makes him/her the original.

If you do not spend enough time with the most important person in your life, the child will not experience a healthy relationship between his or her parents; not to mention, it may end unexpectedly. This is not to say necessarily that you should spend more time with your spouse than your child. It is to say, you are not to neglect the time you used to spend, continue to spend and should be spending with your spouse.

Ultimately, time with your spouse is of the utmost importance, and you both have to work together to make it happen. Remember, you are both one unit. You function as one. Your child comes first to you as a couple. It is important you plan and agree on everything involving your child as much as possible with the exception of the obvious. This will make for a solid relationship. You will have roadblocks either way, but you will likely have a ton fewer than those that do the opposite of this.

At the start of chapter five I wrote about the beginning, the very things you did at the start of your courtship and how adhesively close you were. Not only should you be closer at this point, but a heap happier as well.

Maybe your question is "how do we spend that kind of time together" now that there are children in your lives? Excuses, excuses … You would take off early from work to spend time with your girlfriend/ boyfriend who is now your spouse, but you can't find a way to have time for yourselves now?

Not buying it … If you would just think back, I'm sure there were many other sacrifices made in order to spend time together. Oh, now you've matured and just can't do it anymore. Surely, when I meet the two of you at my seminar in the near future you won't say that to me.

There are circumstances that are an exception. For example, a spouse that travels a large percentage of the time, or one spouse is working nights and the other during the day. These and other circumstances can make time together all the tougher. The average marriage does not have circumstances such as these. Therefore, you should make sure time with your spouse is priority one. In the future, your child will love you more because of it. How can I say that? I'm living proof.

Our children see how close we are, have taken notice of the time we spend together, how much we cherish one another and they've expressed how special that is to them. It also teaches them the value they should put on their future marriage relationship. That alone is an endorsement.

Here are some things you can do together to ensure you spend ample time together.

- From your first child to the last, have a schedule for them. Make sure to stick to it after you both agree to it. Once your newborn gets on a schedule, attempt to keep that schedule until the teen years with slight modifications. As a baby, there will be much more rest than not. As the baby grows older, your schedule must become more routine. If you fail to do this, it will impact the sitter and will totally disrupt opportunities for you and your spouse to have time to be alone.

- If you both work, there are a lot of other opportunities for you to be together. One of the things my wife and I do together (with the exception of what the children are responsible for) is housework. When this is taking place, we are always near one another. Basically, I help with the laundry, our bedroom of course, and the vacuuming. I also cook with my wife and at times prepare the entire meal for the family. Even then, my wife is within earshot and talks to me the whole time.

- Do lawn work together. It's great because we are outside together, and because of that alone we have a wonderful time. Best of all, we are spending time together.

- How about going out on a cool evening and playing a few games of tennis? Take the baby with you if it's within the first year. After that first year when you both are feeling a little more comfortable leaving the baby with a sitter, friends or family, take off for a few hours several times a week and play tennis or other games together.

- How about volleyball? My wife and I love to go out and volley to one another just for fun. Even doing this for an hour is valuable to you as a couple.

- If you don't like to play sports or simply feel non-athletic, then go out to a game together. Now that our children are older we do this quite often. Well, a little bit of both. We like to play sports together, but we also enjoy going out to a sports event together as well.

- Dinner and a movie. Even when your baby is less than a year old this is something you should continue to do. If you've established a sleeping schedule or your child has created one for you, you can still do this. Just go when you know your baby likes to sleep. If you discover movies wake them much too often, that still is not an excuse not to do it. Get a sitter! A sitter does not have to be someone you hardly know. My wife and I would trade off with some of our friends. Sometimes we'd sit for them and vice versa. Family can be called as well.

- One of the things we like to do is visit bookstores. Sometimes we will just go and have dessert while perusing through several books or magazines we may be interested in. At the same time, bookstores give you an opportunity as a couple to enjoy quiet time together. You don't have to be right next to each other. Just knowing you are both there is special.

- When you're driving around in your car, try to remember how talkative you were your first year together. Now what does it seem like? How much does that happen anymore? Talk about whatever is on your mind and do it together even in your car. Sharing your thoughts makes your spouse or companion feel as though you want them to be a part of you. That makes all the difference in the world.

- Most men do not like to go to the grocery store with their wives. I do. Why? Because I'm with my wife. Just another opportunity to spend time with her. If your children are old enough, this shouldn't be a problem at all. You may even have a child old enough to watch over the other children. Why not, I did it for my parents and my wife for hers. Besides, it gives your oldest child the chance to show how responsible they can be.

- My wife is so good at card games, I told her she was born with a deck of cards in her hand. There are a great number of card games that can be played between the two of you. Cribbage is a favorite we love to play. I'm sure you have your own. Either way, it's a fun thing to do when your baby is resting. Oh, I know you have things to do around or outside the house. Still, make time for your spouse. Always ...

- When is the last time you took your wife to a play or a comedy show? All right, maybe it's not for some of you, but it is an idea. The day after you've had it tough at work is a good time to get out and go to a comedy show. <u>Phantom of the Opera</u>, <u>Stomp</u>, <u>Thoroughly Modern Millie</u>, <u>Fiddler on the Roof</u>, and <u>Mamma Mia</u> are some wonderful events to go to along with a great number of others.

- Ever thought about being spontaneous and taking a weekend trip? I'm sure there are many places the two of you would love to go. Get a sitter and leave. Your weekend trip could include a picnic at the park, a barefoot walk out on the beach, a fine dinner, a cabin or hotel stay, a blanket under the stars at midnight or simply a drive with destination stops and scenic views. You can't go wrong here.

- Rent a Limo for the evening. The best time to do something like this does not have to happen during special days in your lives. That's right; you do not need a special reason to rent a limo for the evening. This, of course, is not something everyone can generally afford, which is why I've listed so many other opportunities for you. Save up for it if you need to. I'm not saying it has to be done several times a year. It's a very romantic treat. Enjoy it.

- Visit the Zoo or go to the Circus. The love for animals and their behavior is a relaxing and very enjoyable thing to watch. Yes, I know most people visit the zoo or go to the circus with their children. So what? Where is it written that you can't visit them as a couple? Get out there, be together, and take lots of silly pictures.

These are just some examples of things you can do to spend time together. There are many others I could list but are sure the both of you can come up with other ideas and opportunities to be together. Don't make excuses not to spend time as a couple. Do it as though you've just met. Make concessions for your children, but never neglect each other. You must always remember this.

Your children will see how close you are and have a greater respect for your relationship. Not to mention, they will want to have similar relationships with their companions in the future because of the example you've set. You are number one to your spouse and your spouse is number one to you. One couple functioning as one ... Your children are number one to you both as a couple and as one unit.

I can't express enough the importance of Time with Your Spouse. Hopefully, neither of you will breach the importance of this time. Instead, take full advantage of living your lives to the fullest. When your children are born, you must keep living.

9

Time with Your Child

Spending time with your child is not to be taken for granted. I would imagine most couples do their very best to make sure of this. Even so, the focus of how much time isn't quite as important as the quality of the time we spend with our children. This is really important for the father or mother traveling often and over several days at a time. Unfortunately, there are those couples out there that may be struggling here, and there are bound to be a number of reasons why.

I wrote earlier about several conversations that should take place prior to having a baby. With some couples, it may be a little too late for that, but that does not mean your child or children should ever be neglected of your time. There are many couples I've spoken with (usually consisting of either the male or the female but never both) that have had a tendency to blame the slow progress of their life, loss of their original dreams, and plans for their future, on their children. Blasphemous! If you've got a child or children, let me assure you of something; the only person(s) at fault here is you.

Secondly, children should be at the receiving end of love and attention and plenty of it to boot. This is why you had nine months to prepare. O.K., some of you may not have gone full term. Still, you've had enough time to prepare and by so doing should have a mental map that assists in making sure your children have ample time with both of you. If you are not doing it, I promised you earlier that society will. When that happens, your children will make you wish you would have spent more time with them. It's not worth it nor should that be the conditional reason to spend time with your child. Do it because you want to. Do it because you should.

Basically, my wife and I have set times for our children. Our son is almost eighteen and our daughter is thirteen. When they were babies, we never stopped doing the things we did before our children came. We may not have done it as often initially, but we could hardly tell the difference.

Nevertheless, we always did things with our children and still do to this very day. It never hurts to plan your weeks. It seems we've always had busy weeks. That has never stopped us though. When we schedule our weeks (as we did in the beginning) there is always time for our children on everyday of the week in some capacity or another and there are many places and things to see. We live in an area where there are endless things to do.

Now that our children are older, we literally have a schedule that keeps us close as a family and I always carefully explain this to our children. While they may not fully grasp our motivation now, they will really appreciate it in the future.

During the week our kids are with us Monday through Thursday. Yes, they play with their friends too, but when I get home from work, all friends have to go. We eat together, read a story as family, do something individually for personal progress, pray together as a family, hug one another and prepare for bed. All morning Saturday and all day Saturday, we are with our children the entire day out doing something together. On Saturday evening, our kids are out with friends. While they are out with friends, we go out too. On Sunday, the family is together the whole time. No friends of ours or the children's come over on Sunday. Sunday is totally family time.

As your children grow up and progress in life and experience what life has to offer, it is critical that you become creative with how you plan to spend time with them. Technology for example has changed the way we live and has given our children access to things we never imagined in our day. Because of this, you either need to learn to play Nintendo, Xbox, Sony Play Station, or Game Cube as my wife and I did or lose time with your children. The latter is not acceptable.

There are a great number of couples that are using such technology to baby-sit their children. Let me warn you, get involved, because this game technology will teach your kids some things you'd rather they didn't learn. Your only option here is to become a part of the action, play with them and disallow games that could very well become harmful. Remember, children are a product of their environment. Simply living under the assumption that your children won't be affected is a fallacy in and of itself.

It is utterly important to be as involved with your children as possible. There will always be time to talk if you make time. We know our children want to be with friends and we make sure they have that time. On the contrary, balance is also required here. As their parents, you and your spouse are the governors of that balance.

Our lives have become more complex and congested. I know how hard it may appear at times to spend quality time. It must be done. You absolutely must find time. Never leave anything to chance, particularly your children. Here are some things you can do to ensure you spend ample time with your children:

- **Plan on it**: As I said before, it never hurts to plan. Make sure you are planning enough time each day for your children. They're counting on it.

- **Video Record**: Spend time recording while attending events. Afterwards, spend time on viewing those tapes when you've got nothing better to do. Even if you think the little one is too small to understand what they are looking at, still do it. Not to mention the cherished moments you'll create by doing so.

- **Fruit Tree Picking**: Have any fruit trees in your yard? If so, spend some time picking fruit together with the little ones. It's always fun. If you don't have a fruit tree, there should be many other fruit picking opportunities somewhere around the city if you live in an area where the soil is good enough.

- **Ride Go Carts**: If your children are old enough and tall enough, you can take the whole family to the go cart riding spot nearest you. It's a blast! My kids love it and your kids will too if you haven't scared them half to death with your own driving. Believe it or not, there are a few kids that are afraid of getting on a go cart because of car experiences they've had. If you can get them on it though, they will have much fun. Try it.

- **Go Swimming**: When the time of year permits, swimming is a fun time especially when you're taking your child or children with you. Once there, you can play chase in the shallow depths, play water polo, volleyball, or even see who can spend the most time under water with just one breath. This is another one of those family events I think is so much fun.

- **Picnic in the Park:** Put a basket of sandwiches, chips, soft drinks, a few slices of fruit and a couple of blankets together along with some umbrellas and load into the car. Most parks have ducks so take some old bread or stale crackers with you. Kids love caring for animals and if they are afraid of them they will learn not to be once they see mom and dad doing it for a while. There are usually barbeque pits around also. Bring fresh meat with you if you plan on making a family day of it.

- **Play Laser Tag:** This is fun for the whole family as well. Don't just take your children to play, play with them. If you absolutely have no idea what this game is, ask your children from around ages ten to sixteen. If they don't know anything about it, they will look into it for you. Better yet, just surprise them. Load them up and take a drive. When they ask where you are going, don't tell them. When you get there, what a joy it will be.

- **Go to an Air Show:** This type of family outing is very fun for me given I love aircraft. If you start early enough at anything with your children, they will love whatever it is just as much as you do later in their life. Well, not all children. But, if they see how excited and passionate you are about it, it may become an event that is planned every season.

- **Visit a Pet Store:** This one has always been fun. Children love animals and are almost always trying to pick them up or feed them. Depending on the age, your children will love to do this together with you. This is one of those outings that are best begun at an early age. Once your children are teenagers, they usually would prefer other things if you wait too long to expose them to the pet store.

- **Play Hide and Seek:** One of the original past times. From simply covering your face with a pillow when they are only one or two years old to actually running away to hide in the preteen years. This fun family time game is one that will forever be a part of every family at some capacity or another. Most teens don't care to do this too much with mom and dad. It's still fun all the way up to age twelve in most families.

- **Go to the Beach:** According to my wife, there is nothing like soft white sand on or under your feet. No matter what, the beach is a very relaxing place for the two of you and a great deal of fun for your children. Many games can be played at the beach. One of the fun things to do with really little ones is to build castles or simple bucket shapes. Whatever you chose to do at the beach will be a wonderful time.

- **Supporting Children in Sports or Activities:** Not only is this really fun and time well spent, it's a time your children basically expect of you. There will be times work will get in the way. I caution you here though. If you make plans to make it and promise you'll be there, you should be there. Otherwise, make sure to explain why you can't make it instead of taking that risk. It will still be disappointing, but not to the degree of a broken promise.

- **Ice or Roller Skating:** How's your balance? My wife and I actually met at a roller skating rink over twenty years ago. We still love skating today. Taking our children to the skating rink has always been fun. They really love it. Now, they go out to the rink with their friends two to three times a month. Like I said before, start them early enough in anything and most of the time they will come to love as you do.

- **Go to a Museum:** If you want to have an opportunity to learn some things you missed and stimulate the young minds of your little ones, a museum is the perfect outing for the family. In fact, there are a multitude of educational experiences out there like natural science, history, war, and dinosaur exploration to name a few.

- **The Trampoline:** You're not scared of heights are you? Then get on the trampoline with your children! Oh, I know! I've heard all the excuses. This is broke and that is broke and still hasn't healed yet. Sure … Well, if you really are just too scared to get up there when your children are on it, pull up a couple of chairs, bring a good book with you and cheer them on from time to time. Either way, you're still with them. It's just more fun to actually be on the trampoline. At least to your children it is.

- **Take them Fishing and Camping:** I'm not a very good fisherman, but I don't use that as an excuse. Camping is something we love to do, but we're not what some would consider real campers given we like to retire in a cabin with soft mattresses at bedtime.

While there are many other things you can do to spend time with your child or children, I just wanted to give you an idea of some of the things we do with ours. Yes, we still do them and many other events and outings as well.

The premise here is to establish the importance of quality time and to stress the value of making time for your children. The impact is phenomenal. There will be instances because of work or other reasons that only one of you will be doing these things from time to time. Even so, try your best to be with your children together as much as possible.

Our basic rule is simple. If we are both home, we do it all as a family. Create what is best suited for your family. When you do, stick to it.

10

Establishing Balance, Boundaries and Responsibility

One of the main conflicts between two people in a marriage is the ability to establish, create, instill, uphold, enforce, compromise, communicate, or fully agree to guidelines and standards designed to promote the best possible development and preparation for the future of their children. It is in fact an almost silent phenomenon. Underneath it all, is a tremendous struggle to grasp the extremely important attributes that should naturally fall into alignment here.

Unfortunately, these struggles permeate couples to the point they would much rather fight or disagree than to do what is best for the children. Why is there so many that are more interested in winning an argument and embracing self gratification? When we've chosen to become one, we must also choose to function as one. Not suggesting you have to have a joint bank account as my wife and I do. Jointly, as related to your children, you must function as one. There's absolutely no way the two of you will ever understand this chapter until you realize that.

The two of you can be and will be (if you are not careful) pulled completely apart by not understanding the extreme importance of balance, boundaries and responsibility. Even if you did truly understand, that is only the first step. The next step is ten times harder for most couples in our day particularly. Children are a product of their environment and thus a product of the example you choose to be for them. If the two of you appear confused and fragmented, the children will take notice and call it normal.

Before we can establish, create, instill, uphold, enforce, compromise, communicate, or fully agree to guidelines and standards designed to promote the best possible development and preparation for the future of our children we must first do what? Answer ... Make undoubtedly sure that we as their parents are first and foremost ourselves Accountable and Responsible. Without these two primary attributes, boundaries and balance are absolutely impossible to establish for our children.

Much has changed since the time we were born. Now there is a new word in order. That word is, adjust. Essentially throughout your life as an adult you will hear your children say things like Mom and Dad, "Times have changed". Things are hip now that were not hip during your childhood. This is why the new word "adjust" is so important today. Specifically, to adjust is to amend, change, modify, alter, regulate or correct. As parents we must have our own way of dealing with the times as we grow older and raise children.

We don't have to compromise our beliefs or ethics. As new dangers or temptations become more available to our children, we must stand at the ready to modify, amend, change, alter, regulate or correct. For every new threat, we must be prepared to make adjustments as warranted and without reservation.

Even so, the initial stages are the most critical in any case. In other words, many couples wait much to long to initiate or enforce the rules of accountability and responsibility. Worse than that, the ability to stay consistent is practically non-existent in present day parenting. Boundaries, particularly today, are an absolute must and are to be taken very seriously. If you are attuned to what encircles you and your family in society or otherwise, then you know exactly what I am saying here. If you don't know, it's time to stop living in a box.

So, have the two of you spent ample time deciding how you intend to teach accountability and responsibility to your children? If not, it needs to happen quickly. If your child or children has become a teen already, I will have much greater tools for you in my next book **A Society of Pacification**. In the meantime, there are some very valuable things you will learn in this chapter that should be retroactively applicable.

The one word children have tremendous trouble understanding today is—privilege. Seems strange doesn't it? Well, it's not. The reason the word privilege is so foreign to children today is because most of them are led to believe (by the actions of the parents) that they (the children) are owed everything. Indeed, they are made to believe they don't have to do anything in exchange for what they want which is a fallacy on the part of the parent(s).

The very small percentage of parents charging their child or children with accountability and responsibility from the early stages has had very little to no problem whatsoever creating boundaries or enforcing them for that matter. The reason for this is simple. Remember, children are a product of their environment. **It all starts in the home.** Thus, the earlier they are taught and held accountable and responsible the easier it will be to establish boundaries and balance.

Basically, if you prepare before the birth of your child, there could only be one other issue here. Consistency ... Another key attribute to sending a very profound message that breeds solidarity between Mom and Dad. Again, this is a very critical connection for your children to see. The end result is impressive if you stick to it.

Both of you come from different backgrounds. Be careful to explore your parents' past behaviors and adopt the ones you feel are best suited for your own children. Along with what knowledge you already have, coupled with what you have read here, you will accomplish raising children that know what to expect from you. They will be more accountable and responsible and will be prepared for boundaries that will almost always be subject to change.

So, what do you feel is needed in order to pull this off effectively? Answer … Your ability to communicate well … As I've said numerous times before, it is absolutely imperative that discussions between the two of you take place early. Disagreements must be ironed out and compromise sealed in agreement prior to outlining accountabilities, responsibilities and setting boundaries which ultimately brings forth balance in the home.

Discuss at length how you intend to address accountability and responsibility with your children. Do it together. This conversation will not only build and establish values in your children; it will give them a sense of appreciation relative to their ability to **earn privileges**.

As I said earlier, we must first and foremost, ourselves, by example, show Accountability and Responsibility. In the early stages, children are very visual learners. There will be things you will do throughout the day that you must be mindful of if you already have children in the home. If they are very young, you are being watched. If they are already talking and walking, they are watching and listening very closely.

I cannot emphasize enough the importance of this chapter. I do understand every home situation and background is different and this is precisely the reason for the emphasis here. Now I will share one of the most common situations my research has exposed that is caused by disconnected parents.

Case in Point … Here is a situation that as I said before will cause much confusion for the child, and contention in the marriage.

A good number of couples I've interviewed over the years have shown either parent at one time or another have been at home while the other works. Yes, in our day, the father in some situations is the one at home while the mother works to provide for the family.

Given such an instance, a greater majority of the mothers that do work while the fathers tend to the home expect the same from the father that he would expect from her if he were working. In other words, if the father is a stay at home dad, he needs to ensure that the house, the laundry, the cooking, cleaning, getting the kids off to school and holding the children accountable for their responsibilities are taken care of. Period ...

In this situation, Danny did some of the chores some of the time and cooked some of the time, but that was about it. Gwen had always assigned particular responsibilities to their three children and expected Danny as her supporter and the children's father to hold them accountable. Gwen was always good to tell Danny each day what she'd assigned to each child for the day. Before she left for work, Gwen was sure to remind Danny that before the children were allowed to do anything else, their chores must be completed.

Danny was a much laid back kind of fellow. He never really took anything serious in life and enforced accountability maybe twice a week. This caused much contention in the heart of the Gwen. She never really got angry at him, but generally expressed her displeasure with his inability to be consistent. This also made Gwen feel unappreciated.

Most days of the week, Gwen would come home and the children were down the street with friends or out to a movie or at the park. She had always hoped Danny would have the kids return home for dinner when she arrived as she was on the same schedule every week. Gwen believed in family, and wanted the family together for supper. She had no problem allowing the children out once again to play after the family had supper together. As it was, supper together as a family happened once a week.

Taking a tour of the home to inspect the chores assigned, Gwen found that the rooms of every child were a filthy mess, the bathrooms were still a mess and the dishes were strewn all over the house still from the day before. Gwen says little to nothing to Danny at this time. She's too angry and disappointed. Gwen's waiting for the children to arrive. When they return home she will unleash her displeasure to them and possibly ground every single one of them. Why?

As far as the children are concerned, Danny said it was all right to go and play. As far as the children are concerned, Danny does not care what they are doing or where they are from hour to hour. The children never ask him if they can do anything. They just simply tell him where they are going and Danny's' response is always—o.k.

As soon as Danny hears Gwen pull up in the car, he remembers all that she'd asked him to do. Too late! Once the children arrive home, Gwen digs in deep and they are lectured and grounded. She doesn't care that Danny didn't do his part. Gwen feels they are old enough to be responsible and should know by now what is expected of them. To a certain point Gwen is right. The only problem is, the children are not taught the same principles of accountability and responsibility from their father Danny.

Now, what are the problems with this situation? Will the kids be confused? Are the parents unified in their beliefs about earned privileges versus unearned privileges? Whom will the children side with? The dad of course, because he is their scapegoat and his laid back nature appeals to them. His way does not enforce what mom feels is important for the children.

At this point, is it possible that you have a better understanding of what I mean when I say—**Your spouse comes first or the relationship dies?** Your children come first in your lives together as one unit. Although neither of you may intend to make your spouse feel as though they are last, the situation I just shared would clearly paint such a picture.

If you are not married yet, take some time to think about how important it is to create balance in the family. Write it down and discuss it A.S.A.P. If you are single, make sure to use the compatibility assessment tools. Also ask additional questions you feel are important to you.

Most importantly, insist that privileges are earned by holding your children accountable for their responsibilities. Set boundaries that are upheld and enforced. Children like to know what boundaries they have. It gives them a guide to work with. Be careful never to threaten consequences without following through. **Be consistent.**

In my home, our children were taught very early that they have agency and may choose to do the opposite of what we taught them at any given time. At the same time, they were also cautioned and reminded that as sure as they have a right to make decisions for themselves; they have no say in the consequence(s) as a result of their decision(s).

Become one. Your children will have a much deeper respect for you. Be willing to adjust as necessary. Remember, consistency is the key.

11

For Husbands

What I will attempt to do here is to share the feelings of thousands of women both young and old alike of which I've personally interviewed over the course of the past twenty-plus years. The information I will share at this time are the elements or core of the conversations I feel are viably important for all husbands to be aware of.

Many of your wives have most probably shared some of this information from time to time. The question is; are you listening to her? For now, I want you to read the following and please do your very best to adopt these considerations as soon as humanly possible. Read on ...

Although you've come to learn much in your life about women, society, politics, and a host of hundreds of other subject matter, never are we as husbands to believe we fully understand every need and thought process of our good wives. No mortal is that perfect. On the other hand, there are things within our control, and if those things are handled effectively, you will always be in the winners circle with your wife.

We should do our best at all times to avoid our competitive nature particularly when communicating or discussing issues or concerns she may have. It is required of us today to be more sensitive to their feelings, and we should be. This is just another humble way of telling her you love her.

It is required of us to be more caring and showing it by our actions. Show that you love her by telling her at least once a day and do it from the heart. We married our wives hopefully for what's in their hearts and in their minds. I know I did. We should be careful to treat them with the utmost respect and honor them lifelong.

Life may appear rough at times. Weather the storm, it's worth it. For every day you feel you just can't take it anymore, try to understand that it is also a day for growth and good. Up to this point, I'm sure life has been a challenge. If you are reading this book prior to marriage you will still have challenges in life, but far fewer if you have embraced the content here.

Always understand that you are expected to be the primary provider. This is not the case in all relationships, but it is in most. Taking care of the family from a financial standpoint should never be looked upon as a burden. In fact, it is a joy. As long as you look at it in this way you will also enjoy doing it. Focus on being considerate when your wife wants to talk about something she feels she's struggling with. By that I mean, do your best to avoid fixing everything she talks to you about. It is our nature to react in such a way. In the early stages of my marriage, I had a hard time doing this, but have learned the value of offering a solution only when asked.

Help with the children as much as possible. Be there for your wife. Be the supporting arm she expects you to be. Some wives would insist on handling the children themselves. You should insist on being a part of it. You are an intricate part of your children's lives. If left out, the growth process becomes fragmented. To be as one means to function as one, and to function as one you must work together at raising the family to the point that when your wife speaks, the children know for certain that you are speaking as well.

Do your part in making sure you are a role model for your sons in a positive way conducive to the way you and your wife believes it should be. This is something that should be discussed between your wife and yourself prior to the birth of your son. Why? Because her opinion matters most.

She is number one, and if you disagree with what she thinks a fatherly role model should be or if you feel it conflicts with what you believe and there is no possible compromise, you should probably choose another partner. It's that simple. Remember, getting married knowing there will be no compromise in areas you are already aware of is only a path to separation or divorce sooner or later.

To most of your wives, the way you treat her in the presence of your sons is important. She knows it will impact him and he will follow you. If you yell and scream at her, your son thinks this is how it should be and he will emulate your actions by recording them for use later on. Don't doubt it …

Our daughters are as precious as their mothers and are to be treated as such. Daughters close to their fathers are most likely to avoid seeking the wrong type of attention outside of the home. The basic message on daughters is to be as close to her as you would your son. Show them equal love and attention. Spend a good amount of time with her. Have a father-daughter date at times when she is the only one you spend time with for the greater part of the day.

This type of bonded relationship is essential in our world today. The more your daughters know you are there for them and can talk to you the safer they will feel.

Choose friends that are married and actually believe in marriage. Some friends have a tendency to coerce with ill intent and disregard the sacred marriage you have. Avoid such friends of negative influence. These are also the friends that choose to go to the outer boundaries when feuding with their companion. Your wife would rather you stayed away from such people.

Give your wife a break by taking all the children out for the day. If she home-schools, she will really appreciate it. Even so, there are those days when our wives feel overwhelmed. Those are the days to give her peace, rest and solace.

With your children, be as gentle with your tone as possible. There will be times you will have to reprove with sharpness, but show forth love even greater afterwards. The fact that you are a man already enhances your message by your physical presence and the natural tone of your voice. If you are consistent, your natural tone will be enough.

Although I am encouraging you to be gentle, this does not remove you from doing your part in holding your children accountable for their responsibilities. Make sure to establish rules and boundaries best suited for your children as it is different in every family.

Give them agency, but if the lines are crossed, be ready to deal with it accordingly. Many times that means you have to remove a certain level of trust. We never want to restrict our children from going out and having fun, but if we find that their hearts are in the wrong place and could be a danger or a threat to them or to your neighbors' children, agency and trust must be limited for a time.

The choices your children make are always all right until they become a danger or a threat. You cannot and should not support agency for the sake of the happiness of your child under circumstances that are critical or harmful in nature. At that time, agency becomes a privilege.

Question, do we all have agency? Are there policemen in our city? Are there judges in our country? Get the message? Agency is a rightful privilege until violations occur.

Be willing to help around the house as needed. If you sense things are getting out of hand, do your best not to complain. The impact of being silent and the family taking notice to you doing chores they are generally charged with not only sets a good example, it also brings about guilt and they join in. If this is something you have to do much more often than not, you will need to implement consequences. If you take away something your children love to do, that usually remedies irresponsibility.

Always do your very best to make time for your wife. Do not make excuses as to why you can't. Given she's the most important person in your life, you must never neglect her. This is why my wife and I have date night every Friday without exception. If Friday is not a good night because of a function you intend to support for your children, then go together and have some alone time on Saturday.

Help to teach the children to respect other adults and to use respectful language not only in their (other parents/adults) presence, but at all times. It is also important (particularly today) to teach our children to respond without using words like—"What?" "Huh?" Or, "say what?" Moms may not mention it to you, but they really appreciate a child that responds respectfully.

As fathers, we can also help by insisting that our adult friends and neighbors are never addressed by their first names. This is unacceptable, and if accepted by your friends or neighbors', you should insist that it is not acceptable in your family. Besides, if your friends and neighbors' accept such disrespect, it makes the children feel they are on the same adult level. Help to support raising respectable children by demanding respect from your own children first.

Although we (men) personally have a list of our own problems and challenges, it is absolutely imperative that we spend a great deal of time giving praise. I know that can be hard at times, but there is great joy in seeking out the best attributes, talents and gifts our wives are blessed with. Take time to recognize the good things she does that makes your life better. Even if it has nothing to do with you, there is always something you can take a moment to compliment her about.

Spend more time being affectionate. Cuddle more at different times of the day. Surprise her by holding her hand while out in public, particularly if it is something you never do or have never done. You will be amazed at the results. Her face will light up.

Send flowers at non-celebrated times or dates. Don't wait for her birthday, mother's day or your anniversary. Send flowers on a day she would least expect them. Don't wait until after an argument. Sure that's always a good time to send them, but not near as special as a total surprise. When you know she's had a rough day, offer to bring dinner home. She will be thankful.

Listen ... The most important concern I think I've ever heard has always been a husband's inability to listen. Listen to her as though your life depended on it. Although there are many keys to a successful relationship, the ability to listen is one of the major ones.

Our wives go through or are responsible for a great deal more than we are. I personally believe that to be true. When the scales are actually balanced, their loads are much heavier in the grand scheme of things. Be cognizant of that by giving her the support, care, nurturing love, and consideration she rightfully deserves.

If you are stuck and in a position where you're having a hard time understanding what is wrong and it isn't anything I've covered here, you might want to take a moment with your wife. Most of all, remember that **<u>your wife is always first and should be acknowledged and treated as such</u>**. Good luck gentlemen ...

12

For Wives

What I will attempt to do here is to share the feelings of thousands of men both young and old alike of which I've personally interviewed over the course of the past twenty-plus years. The information I will share at this time are the elements or core of the conversations I feel are viably important for all wives to be aware of.

I should only hope I do not appear biased when I say, I believe most women are truly and undoubtedly the hardest working beings on the face of our great planet. You honestly go through much more than men do, and your challenges are far greater. A great number of you (even though times have changed) are still at home with the children for the better part of the day and if you work, you still are with your children more than your husband on average.

What may be hard for you to understand is time with you, even after the first child is born, is more important to your husband than he may ever choose to share with you. Because of this, it is also important to understand that all men at some point or another were also nurtured by a mom. The fact is, we never forget that, and to some degree will always need to have it even if it means getting it from you. I'm specifically talking about nurturing care, understanding and reflection.

Although you've come to learn much in your life about men, society, politics, and a host of hundreds of other subject matters, never are you as wives to believe you fully understand every need and thought process of your good husbands. No mortal is that perfect. On the other hand, there are things within your control, and if those things are handled effectively, you will always be in the winners circle with your husband.

Make time for him. Do your very best to make sure that you are making attempts to spend quality time with him. This should be done whether there are children in the home or not. Remember, your husband is priority one. As a couple functioning as one, the children come first, but never before your husband.

Here's the reason why. There are many couples out there that ignore the very importance of this message and some make it right up until the last child has left the home. Sounds good right? Wrong ... Soon after, a divorce takes place and the spouse that chose to neglect is in deep shock when they discover that the only reason the neglected stayed in the marriage was for the sake of the children and nothing more. The basic consensus is, "you were not there for me then, so why should I be here for you now?".

In other cases, I've personally met both men and women that have been through this and accepted a miserable relationship right up to the time the last child was gone. In most other cases the split takes place before the children leave.

Don't be fooled into thinking this could not happen to you, or that your husband would never ever do such a thing. Instead, choose to make him the priority and the children will always be priority to the both of you as one unit.

One of the best things that could ever touch the hearts of husbands is the feeling of appreciation. If you are a stay at home mom, try to keep tidy. One of the complaints I've always heard is, he's worked hard all day and comes home to a disaster. If you don't keep a neat and organized home, a great deal of husbands take offense to it and feel unappreciated. Again, if you are a stay at home mom, please keep tidy. It matters to your husband.

You've heard the saying that the way to the heart of the man is through his stomach. They ought to carve that in stone somewhere. It's true … Although it's not everything, it is true. This is another one of those, when I come home from work type complaints. If you both work, there should clearly be a compromise. Otherwise, if you're at home and he is the sole provider, he more than likely would like something prepared for him. The opposite is also true.

It is true that most men naturally expect moms to be the primary nurturer of the children. It is also true that your husbands expect you to be on the same page as he. By that I mean, when two parents are unified and agree on how to raise the children, the bond is strong and virtually tamper proof.

There will be times you and your husband will need to make modifications. That is only normal. You know you are solid in your communications with your children when you speak and they know your husband is also speaking even though he may not be present.

While it is very important the children see you as the primary nurturer, it does not limit you to being a disciplinarian as well. Why should you be the primary nurturer? There is nothing better than the love and affection of a mom.

I know how hard it can be for moms trying to create balance in the way they communicate with children and shifting between nurturer and disciplinarian. In our day and time, this balance is absolutely essential not only for the love of our children but for their safety as well.

Make sure to establish rules and boundaries best suited for your children as it is different in every family. Give them agency, but if the lines are crossed be ready to deal with it accordingly. Many times that means you have to remove a certain level of trust. We never want to restrict our children from going out and having fun, but if we find that their hearts are in the wrong place and could be a danger or a threat to them or to your neighbors' children, agency and trust must be limited for a time.

The choices your children make are always all right until they become a danger or a threat. You cannot and should not support agency for the sake of the happiness of your child under circumstances that are critical or harmful in nature. At that time, agency becomes a privilege.

Question, do we all have agency? Are there policemen in our city? Are there judges in our country? Get the message? Agency is a rightful privilege until violations occur.

Help your husband in making sure to hold the children accountable for their responsibilities. There is only one way to do this and that is to **be consistent**. If you are one that allows them to get away with things you generally wouldn't when their dad is home, it will surely cause confusion and chaos. Situations like this not only disrupt the progression of the marriage, it also tells the children they can cause conflict between you and your spouse.

Make sure that you discuss with your husband decisions you plan to make concerning your children particularly if it involves money. Set a certain amount you both agree would be all right under normal circumstances.

The reason for this is your husband may already have plans for a surprise vacation or something else planned for the family or an anniversary celebration. When attempting to debit the account, he ends up short. That usually doesn't make for a great afternoon when he gets home. Maybe this is something that never happens in your home. If it isn't, you're in good shape.

Unless you always want your husband to go out to sporting events with his friends, it would be great if you would not only go with him (even if you don't really care for the event/sport) to these games at times, it would be even better if you suggested it. I've heard many complaints about wives complaining that their husbands are going out to events/sports with friends and not taking them along. That should not be … It is best that it's the two of you rather than seven of his friends. Offer to go out to sporting events with him. He'll just love it.

Choose friends that are married and actually believe in marriage. Some friends have a tendency to coerce with ill intent and disregard the sacred marriage you have. Avoid such friends of negative influence. These are also the friends that choose to go to the outer boundaries when feuding with their companion. Your husband would rather you stayed away from such people.

Do your best to avoid badgering your husband about his day or insisting he talks about it. While it would be nice if he would, most men have a hard time going through their entire day when they get home. Give him some breathing room. At a time when you're not anxious and he's talking a bit, let him know that you'd like to be apart of his day when he gets home.

Please do not deny physical attention as a means to manipulate. This type of neglect is one of the absolute worst for your husbands and one that could cause major problems in your marriage. Of course, there are exceptions such as the natural time of the month, pain caused by a fall or an accident, being sick and etc … There are many other good excuses I'm sure, but if you're consistently denying physical attention, there will more than likely be some major issues brewing.

When times are tough, it is utterly important that full support is rendered. Many of your husbands take their role as the provider very seriously. The last thing he needs is to be beaten while you're in financial dire straights. If you are married and reading this, please, do your best to remember your sacred vows and oaths at the altar. If I remember correctly, I could have sworn I heard the words—"For Richer or For Poorer".

Sometimes we make decisions that test the fibers of our marriage. Other times we may lose our jobs. In this life, nothing is certain. Don't let him down. Support him and encourage him. Insist that you know everything will be just fine.

Your reward, he'll bounce back much quicker than you think. Kicking him while he's down will only make matters worse and/or extend his unemployment status. The reason for this is his morale will be down at this point already. He will need you to lift that morale up.

If you are stuck and in a position where you're having a hard time understanding what is wrong and it isn't anything I've covered here, you might want to take a moment with your husband. Most of all, remember that your husband is always first and should be acknowledged and treated as such. Good luck ladies …

13

Keeping the Marriage Alive

If you have read this book thoroughly up to this point, you will have a greater understanding of this conclusion.

It is my only hope and prayer that you would utilize the tools I've given here. These are down to earth real world issues, circumstances, and situations that broaden our ability to have the strongest possible marriage. While trial and error are the norm, what I've attempted to do here is provide reality, caution and tools that will ultimately limit and minimize trauma within your relationship.

As I've said a great number of times throughout this book, "Your Spouse is Priority One". If you embrace that, you will be in good shape for as long as you both shall live. To place an even higher emphasis on this message, do your best to remember, **"Your Children will Leave"**. When that happens, your bond is to be solid and without resentment.

Divorce in our country is nearly fifty percent and a significant number of those unfortunate happenings take place after the children have all left the home. You did not plan to get married, raise children, and lose your spouse. No one plans such an ending devastation. However, it is evidently clear that every relationship requires effort.

In order to keep the marriage alive, the effort must be jointly exercised in every aspect of your relationship. You must truly do your very best to realize the importance of oneness while making sure to have balance without chaos. This can be tricky but, if you work on it diligently, you will do just fine.

Each day we are blessed to wake up brings forth new challenges designed to test us and our families. As long as the both of you are readily at the helm and quick to praise rather than find fault, you will overcome such challenges.

Another great tool you can use is the 80/20 rule. In practically every relationship before marriage and after, you have found that the reason you stayed with this person or married them is because the good in him or her clearly outweighed the bad. In other words, in the beginning you didn't have to work so hard to recognize the great benefits he or she had to offer. Nor did you spend a great amount of time focusing on what was not such a great benefit. For this reason, you are now married and I'm sure the benefits are still greater.

So, what exactly is the 80/20 rule? It is to have the ability within yourself to focus 80 percent of your energy on the wonderful things about your spouse or partner. The other 20 percent should almost never surface verbally unless it becomes a habit that threatens life. This isn't to say you should ignore wrongdoing or abuse.

There will almost always be something in your relationship about him or her that you don't exactly care for. The question is, did you know this prior to becoming deeply involved? If the answer is yes, and most times it is, then do your very best not to harbor ill feelings towards them. Instead, focus on the 80 percent that committed you to the relationship.

Likewise, the courtship should never end. Be sure to plan at least one day a week to spend some real quality time together "**without the children**". Date nights are something that most likely happened often in the beginning. Do not allow anything to change that now. Excuses will not suffice! If there is a will—there is a way. Make sure there is a will. No exceptions …

Be as thoughtful as possible by consciously considering how your partner may feel about a decision you intend to make. If this simple practice is exercised throughout your relationship, you will successfully avoid arguments that should have never happened in the first place. Usually, these are money decisions, but there are others. If you know your partner well enough, common sense should prevail here.

Indeed, you have a solemn duty to make sure your children see the unity within your relationship with your spouse and it does not end there. Your child or children need also to experience unity by the affection you openly display in their presence. In essence, unity is oneness. Your children will understand this clearly when they realize you are joined at the hip as a couple. Ultimately, this is self evident when your children ask Dad a question and conclude that Mom will have the same answer or response to the same question.

I'm not suggesting you shouldn't have different thoughts or opinions. That is what makes us human. On the other hand, there need be little confusion on the stance you take relative to certain situations and opportunities available to your children today. In today's world particularly, parents must be cautious and cognizant, and because of this, we must stand at the ready in unity and oneness.

Furthermore, you must always remember to prioritize the order of your relationship with your children. A clear example of this is mentioned in Chapter 7 with the title ___"Mother, Father and Parent before Friend"___. The first reason I remind you of this is because of the confusion it can cause and the difficulty you will have when attempting to counsel or reprimand your children. Secondly, if only one of you chooses to follow this necessary principle, keeping the marriage alive will be all the more difficult. I have a few questions for you:

- Question 1; Are you perfect?

- Question 2; Are you infallible?

- Question 3; Are there things about you that you aren't happy about?

- Last Question; Are you mistake free, everyday, 100 percent of the time?

Given I could most assuredly answer all four of those questions for you; I should only hope you understand the greater and more essential purpose of **"<u>focusing on you</u>"**.

Too many of us waist time and energy thinking about what someone else did or how you felt they should have said it or done it differently. Yes, of course that would satisfy your purpose, but not anyone else's. Obviously, they felt to react or respond exactly the way they wanted to because of their own reasons or justification. It doesn't mean they were right, nor does it mean you need to fix it.

This is critical because it requires unconditional love. This is also the time you should probably think about your partners' background prior to marriage. Generally, you will realize why he or she said or did it differently than you would have after considering the source of their action(s).

All people are a product of the environment of their up-bringing and the examples set by family and friends along the way. Even so, no one forces us to make the decisions we choose to make as adults.

Remember Chapter 4's "Compatibility Assessment Tools"? Remember the warning I gave you? It says this specifically; "It's decision making time. Ask, why am I doing this? Is this a real match for my future? Am I committed to him or her? Should I settle for a maybe?" After making your compatibility assessment, your ultimate decision is not only a decision; it is your sole commitment. Remember that ...

Obviously, there are many whom were married prior to reading this book. That does not change the perspective of the paragraph above. For that matter, you should do all possible to "Keep the Marriage Alive". You made the decision, now make the best of it.

My wife taught me the following great lesson—"**Do your very best to understand rather than to be understood**".

There are many books out there that will lend reason to what you should do and why, the psychology behind this decision or that, and even pinpoint which side of the brain generated or stimulates a particular behavior or response. I see nothing wrong with reading books of such in-depth understanding and counsel. Those particular books have their own value. Always do all you can to continuously educate yourself no matter the purpose.

Once you have mastered the suggestions I have provided in this book, I recommend that you read my second book, **A Society of Pacification**. That book covers parents of today in more detail, the society which has influenced their behavior, and the consequences of pacifying something they don't honestly believe in, if but only to please their children.

I look forward to personally meeting you at one of my seminars and discussing these and other topics in greater detail.

Have a happy marriage.

978-0-595-44689-6
0-595-44689-2

www.ingramcontent.com/pod-product-compliance
Lightning Source LLC
Chambersburg PA
CBHW030346290526
45785CB00004B/1625